Glimpses of Lincoln, Illinois

*An Inside Look at
Abraham Lincoln's Namesake City
Nestled Along Route 66*

JAN SCHUMACHER

**Foreword by Paul Beaver
Professor Emeritus, Lincoln College**

ISBN: 978-0-9795467-0-9

Printed by Lincoln Printers, Lincoln, Illinois

© 2007 by Jan Schumacher. All rights reserved.

Dedicated to my parents, Art and Mickey Strobel, whose love and encouragement has made all the difference in my life

Contents

Forward vii
Introduction ix
Acknowledgements xi

History

Lincoln: A Man of Humor 3
A. Lincoln in Logan County 7
Sesquicentennial Song 11
Route 66 Mania 15
The Mother Road in Lincoln 19
Preserving the Mill 23
Lure of Route 66 27
LJHS Building 31
Logan County Courthouse 35

Community

Lincoln Experiences 41
Bright Future Ahead 45
Historic Preservation 49
Locally Owned vs. Chain Stores 53
What Newcomers Enjoy 57
Fairs and Festivals 61

Funeral Visitations 65
Christmas Parade 69
Estate Auctions 77
Lincoln Sesquicentennial 81
Being Connected 85
Picturesque Central Illinois 89
Servant Leadership 93
Gut Value Connections 97
Dreams 101

People

Moving Back 107
Tribute to Mike Abbott 111
Special Mothers 115
Memorable Fathers 119
Inspiring Political Figures 123
Sonya Twist Remembered 127
Helping Our Soldiers 131
LCHS Teacher Retirements 135
Stay-at-home Moms 139
Lincoln's "Idols 143
Illinois State Fair 147
Help with Tornado Clean-up 151

For More Information on Lincoln 155

Foreword

Jan Schumacher's work "Glimpses of Lincoln, Illinois" is certainly one of the more unique books I've had the privilege of reading. It is a very entertaining look at the great variety of people who make up our hometown. "Glimpses" truly describes life in Lincoln, Illinois.

Lincoln, with its population of 15,000 lies in the very middle of Illinois, and as in smaller towns everywhere, the people who live here share a wide variety of life experiences. Jan writes of the town's fascinating Abraham Lincoln history and especially of the town's native sons and daughters. She writes of teachers, politicians - some who rose to great heights, and of the town's merchants, lawyers, doctors. Jan tells us about the Balloon Festival, the Route 66 activities, Christmas Parade and many of the other local events.

It is a fun book to read. I know that "Glimpses of Lincoln, Illinois" will prove very enjoyable reading to those of all ages.

Paul J. Beaver
Professor Emeritus
Lincoln College
Lincoln, Illinois

Introduction

Just as snapshots capture a scene by freezing action in the photograph, so these newspaper columns from 2002 to 2007 present a glimpse of Lincoln by using words to describe an aspect of the community at the time they were written. Dates that the columns were published in the Courier appear below their titles.

Lincoln is the quintessential small Midwestern town. From the picturesque courthouse square downtown to the charming historic neighborhoods to the surrounding rich farmland, the city has a Norman Rockwell appearance.

But it's the warm, friendly people committed to their community who make Lincoln special. I've been fortunate to interview many such residents in writing my weekly column. The experience has embedded Lincoln in my heart.

Jan Schumacher
Lincoln, Illinois
April, 2007

Acknowledgements

Thanks to Jeff Nelson, managing editor at The Courier, for giving me the opportunity to write a weekly column. A writer couldn't ask for a better editor.

Special thanks also to my husband, Steve, who is a great proofreader.

Thanks also to the many Courier readers who conveyed their enjoyment of my newspaper columns when they originally appeared.

History

Lincoln: A Man of Humor
January 25, 2003

History is not what you thought. It is what you can remember. W.C. Sellar

We all know Abraham Lincoln was a serious man who wisely and bravely led our country through extremely difficult times. But most folks don't realize what a down-to-earth man he was, one with a great sense of humor.

Accounts of his visits to Logan County round out the picture history paints of this famous man. In the 1911 book "The History of Logan County," author Lawrence Stringer noted, "Other localities may remember Lincoln as the president, the hero of the war, the savior of his country and the martyr to a righteous cause, but to Logan County and central Illinois alone belongs the Lincoln who built his neighbor's cabin, hoed his neighbor's corn and followed a rough justice around a rough circuit."

Lincoln was the personal friend to early settlers of Logan County, visiting their homes, attending to their lawsuits, inspiring them with homespun integrity and entertaining them with his ready jokes, Stringer said.

He relates a story Lincoln was fond of telling about a stay at the Deskins Tavern while in Postville (now Lincoln) for a trial.

"After everybody had gone to bed, there came a terrific pounding at the door. The landlord got up to let in the energetic assailer of the portal, who seemed to be in search of a drink of whiskey.

"The landlord explained he had no whiskey in the house, whereupon the visitor wanted to know if there was any place in the village where a drink could be had. To all these questions, the landlord returned a negative and as the full horrors of his whiskey-less situation burst upon him, the fellow said, with great emotion, "Good heavens! Give me an ear of corn and a tin cup and I'll make it myself."

Stringer relates a more serious account of Lincoln driving back from Postville to Springfield with Judge Treat in the judge's buggy. "While passing along the moonlit road, he saw a polecat in the track before them. Treat was for driving right ahead but Lincoln remarked he had more experience with such matters than the judge, took the lines out of the judge's hand and drove carefully in the timber, making a detour at a safe distance from the animal and then back to the road again.

"On returning the lines to the judge, Lincoln remarked that he had been caught once and had learned, that in some cases, discretion was the better part of valor."

A humorous incident occurred relating to the lot Lincoln owned on the site of the current Sherwin Williams store in downtown Lincoln. He had co-signed a note with his friend James Primm. When Primm was unable to pay the note, Lincoln paid it and Primm deeded him the land to reimburse him.

Lincoln Police Magistrate Lewis Rosenthal related the following 1858 account to Stringer. "Mr. Lincoln came to the courthouse in Lincoln to pay his taxes on the lot. Prior to this visit, I had been living near Mr. Lincoln's lot and the lot being unused, and knowing that Mr. Lincoln would not care, I put up a small temporary shed on his lot and stabled a few extra horses there for a short time. I had never had the opportunity to tell Mr. Lincoln what I had done, not having met him.

"While Rosenthal was preparing the receipt for Lincoln after he paid the taxes, Lincoln happened to look out the window and see the shed on his lot. 'Say, Rosenthal,' said he, 'isn't that my lot over there?' I told him I guessed it was. 'Well, who put that shed up there?' inquired Mr. Lincoln.

"'Well,' I replied, 'a fellow in town here put up that shed but the fellow is a good friend of yours.'

"'That's all right,' said Mr. Lincoln, 'but that fellow, whoever he is, ought to pay my taxes. He is getting all the benefit out of the lot and I get none.'

"'Well,' I replied. 'I know that fellow, Mr. Lincoln and he won't pay a cent.'

"'Well, who is he anyway?' said Mr. Lincoln.

"'If you must know, Mr. Lincoln' I replied, 'I'm the fellow.'

"He looked at me a second or two, and with a twinkle in his eye, said, 'Hand over that receipt. I guess I'm in for it.'"

Another humorous incident occurred in Atlanta on July 4, 1859, when Lincoln was attending a church festival at the new Congregational church.

Stringer relates the account, "During the evening a local baker, James Wren, came forward to present to Mr. Lincoln a cake he had baked for the occasion, but became embarrassed and stood before Mr. Lincoln, holding out the cake, being unable to give an utterance to the little speech he had carefully prepared.

"Lincoln saved the situation by saying to those assembled, 'I'm not so hungry as I look.' This broke the spell and everyone laughed, including the baker."

It was this self-depreciating humor and good nature that endeared Lincoln to so many Logan County residents before he was beloved by an entire nation.

A. Lincoln in Logan County
September 21, 2002

I claim not to have controlled events, but confess plainly that events have controlled me. Abraham Lincoln

How many stories about Abraham Lincoln in Logan County do you know? Most residents have a passing familiarity with the account of Lincoln christening the city with the juice of a watermelon. They know he practiced law at the Postville and Mt. Pulaski courthouses. But they'd be hard pressed to give many details or to name other experiences he had here.

That lack of information is about to change. The local Looking for Lincoln Committee has begun filming an 18-minute video, "From Surveyor to President: A. Lincoln in Logan County." Soon residents and visitors alike will become familiar with local stories about Abraham Lincoln.

Recognizing the truism that a picture is worth a thousand words, we are fortunate to have artist Lloyd

Ostendorf's pictures of various Lincoln scenes in the county to give us an idea of what Abe's experiences here might have looked like.

Certainly the reenactment of the christening scene at the Railsplitter Festival every year has helped familiarize folks with that story.

The novelty of being the only city named for Lincoln before he became president is certainly a claim to fame. But it is a little known fact to most people outside Logan County. Even local schoolchildren who study history as past of their education aren't particularly aware of our Lincoln heritage.

With the completion and distribution of the video, visitors will have the opportunity to see Lincoln stories brought to life. Students will be able to view reenactments at places they see on a regular basis.

When the Looking for Lincoln heritage tourism program was initiated a few years ago, state historians encouraged towns to research and relate the stories of Lincoln in their communities. We were lucky to already have a wealth of information about Lincoln in the county.

Much of the information is from the book of early Logan County history written by Judge Lawrence Stringer. One of the most familiar pieces of information comes from a letter written by John Stevens to Stringer detailing his boyhood memory of the christening.

The video will bring to life incidents here in our backyard involving the beloved 16th president.

Did you know that one of Lincoln's first trips to present-day Logan County was to survey an area on Salt Creek north of Middletown? He did the work for his friend Samuel Musick who wanted to build a ferry or toll bridge on the road between Springfield and Peoria so he could profit from travelers who crossed at that point.

Were you aware that Lincoln stopped at the Stagecoach Inn that was later built near the ferry?

Did you realize that when Lincoln was in town as an attorney traveling the 8th Judicial Circuit, he enjoyed playing town ball and marbles with children in Postville Park? It was even at Postville Courthouse that a judge first referred to Lincoln as "Honest Abe." Of course, he also represented clients in cases at the Mt. Pulaski Courthouse when he was riding the 8th Circuit.

Have you heard about Lincoln staying in a carriage house on the Hoblit farm near Atlanta? The Hoblit home had been destroyed by fire, so the family was staying in the carriage house. They apologized for the uncomfortable sleeping arrangements, but in his gracious way, Lincoln said he was content to have a place to sleep in the company of good friends. Lincoln also spoke at a large Fourth of July celebration in 1859 in Turner's Grove, near the Atlanta Cemetery, where he was presented a gold-headed cane.

Elkhart also has a connection to Lincoln through his friendship with John D. Gillett, whom he visited asking for help in the presidential election and later invited to the inaugural ceremonies in Washington.

Sadly, the last direct connection Logan County had with Lincoln was when his funeral train passed through the county enroute to Springfield, giving residents the opportunity to bid farewell to the man who had influenced so many of their lives.

What a treasure this video will be as it depicts these

and other scenes.

Those involved with the production, from the video company to Looking for Lincoln Chairman Paul Beaver to the many volunteers who appear as extras, are excited to have this opportunity to share our local stories about a local man who rose to greatness.

Sesquicentennial Song
August 30, 2003

What its children become, that will the community become.
                                           Suzanne La Sollette

Talk about expanding education beyond the classroom. Carroll Catholic School students recently had a unique opportunity to do that.

Under the director of their music teacher, Ruth Freesmeier, Carroll students wrote and performed a song for Lincoln's Sesquicentennial.

As part of an annual exercise in composing a song, last year's seventh graders wrote the lyrics to "A Lincoln Sesquicentennial Tribute." The process not only gave them the opportunity to put into practice what they'd learned about such things as note writing and rhythm, it also became a history lesson.

The youngsters researched the city's history for ideas of what to mention in the lyrics. They spent five weeks writing the song.

They'd been learning about the musical partnership

of Richard Rodgers and Oscar Hammerstein, with Hammerstein writing lyrics and Rodgers putting them to music. So sending the lyrics to a composer was a logical step for the students, rather than using a familiar tune.

Jason Yarcho, a 1997 Carroll graduate who is now a music major at Eastern Illinois University, was an ideal choice. When the students heard the music Yarcho composed for their song, they exclaimed, "This sounds like a Broadway show!"

After the song was completed, Freesmeier mentioned to Mayor Beth Davis that the Carroll students would like to perform the song at a City Council meeting during the Sesquicentennial year. But Davis was so impressed with the song, she decided it should be sung at the re-enactment of the christening.

Once those plans were made, Freesmeier taught the song to the fifth through eighth grade students. One girl even took the words home over the summer to practice.

Abbie Feldman, an eighth grader whose great-great grandfather led Lincoln's Centennial parade as mayor of the city, was especially excited to be carrying on the family tradition of participating in the city's anniversary celebrations, Freesmeier said.

As part of the educational process, the students chose to have the song copyrighted, learning how that step protects musicians' interests.

"We've had good feedback on the song," Freesmeier noted. Music definitely added to the Sesquicentennial celebration, making it more colorful, she said.

Here are the lyrics to "A Lincoln Sesquicentennial Tribute", used with Freesmeier's permission.

Back in 1853 when Old Abe named our town,
He poured that watermelon juice right on the ground.
He looked at his friends and neighbors, then exclaimed with glee,
"What a great place this will be to raise a family!"

Our fam'ly tree has many great faces. It has grown so much,
all descendants of good folk like Gillett, Hickox 'n such.
Mr. Latham, Mr. Scully gave us parks to eat our lunch,
to sing and dance and play our games – things we like a bunch.

Lots of schools have sprouted up for sports and learning, too.
We've followed in your footsteps, Abe; we want to be like you!
"Honest, Abe" we read our books and study history.
We play a little baseball, too. We all want to succeed.

Our downtown and our railroad station still are here today.
Some of the stores and business places are still the same old way.
Our courthouse stands and beams with pride, it is the county seat –
judges, lawyers, common folk – it's just the place to meet.

We're in a new millennium. Our lives have changed a lot.
With all our precious memories we can connect the dots.
Though we've said goodbye to gents and wartime veterans,

we're here to say hello to new ones and welcome all our friends.

*O Lincoln, O Lincoln, look at us today.
A 150 years we've come. Oh, celebrate! Hooray!*

"I explained to the students that by writing this song and performing it, they were making history," Freesmeier said. "I told them to keep their copies of the song because they will be in their 60s for the Bicentennial celebration, and the words from the Sesquicentennial song will be very special to them then."

Route 66 Mania
October 5, 2002

Thanks to the Interstate Highway System, it is now possible to travel across the country from coast to coast without seeing anything. Charles Kuralt

A few weeks ago, a Hawaiian man stopped by the Lincoln College Museum after seeing the museum sign on Lincoln Parkway. He had flown into Chicago from Maui and rented a car to drive the entire length of Route 66.

Not long after that, a group of English visitors traveling in their touring cars along Route 66 stopped at Dick Logan's Auto Care Center for directions.

Lincoln has been experiencing just a small part of the Route 66 mania spreading across the globe. This fascination with traveling the famous route has exploded over the last 15 years as people yearn to recreate the experience of driving this historic highway.

Last weekend, 35,000 people celebrated Route 66

nostalgia at the first-ever International Route 66 Mother Road Festival in Springfield. Classic cars, oldies music and Route 66 memorabilia were spread throughout downtown.

What is the attraction of Route 66 to tourists? Perhaps it's because it symbolizes freedom and opportunity. It reminds us of a simpler time.

"This road is a part of the American story," said Jim Conkle, executive director of the Route 66 Preservation Foundation. "Route 66 is just as important as older sites in the East that mark a particular period in American history.

"Families seeking a better life traveled west on Route 66. Veterans seeking jobs in the aerospace industry followed Route 66 to California. And thousands of families spent their summer vacations driving along Route 66," he said.

"It's definitely a piece of Americana worth celebrating today and preserving for tomorrow."

Having recently observed its 75th birthday in 2001, the National Historic Route 66 Federation says Route 66's contributions to the nation must be evaluated in the broader context of American social and cultural history.

U.S. Highway 66 hastened the most comprehensive westward movement and economic growth in U.S. history, the federation says. Like the early long-gone trails of the 19th century, Route 66 helped to spirit of second mass relocation of Americans.

Store owners, motel managers and gas station

attendants recognized early on that even the poorest travelers required food, automobile maintenance and adequate lodging. Just as the New Deal work relief programs provided employment with the construction and maintenance of Route 66, the appearance of countless tourist courts, garages and diners promised sustained economic growth after the road's completion, the federation observed.

Often called the "Main Street of America," Route 66 linked rural communities like Lincoln, Elkhart and Atlanta with two vital 20th century cities — Chicago and Los Angeles.

Originally Route 66 in Lincoln ran along North Kickapoo Street south to Keokuk Street. There it made a brief jog west to Logan Street, following Logan south until the curve where it turned into Fifth Street.

It continued on Fifth Street to Washington Street, at Postville Park, where it turned south. The route left town past The Mill restaurant and Lincoln Developmental Center — known as the Lincoln State School in that era.

By 1939, highway officials decided to reroute Route 66 to a new four-lane beltway around Lincoln to relieve the heavy traffic flow through town. Naturally, downtown business owners were opposed to this idea because they didn't want to lose business, but the highway planners prevailed.

In the 1980's, a group of Illinoisans joined their counterparts in the seven other Route 66 states who were involved with the movement to resurrect the old road, forming the Route 66 Association of Illinois in 1989.

Each year the association sponsors a week-end motor tour between Chicago and St. Louis. The tours stop in 10-12 towns along the way.

Before the tour grew to include 450 people, Lincoln hosted the group for dinner and overnight stays. In the association's Fall 2002 newsletter, a Chicago-area woman recalled her Route 66 Motor Tour to Lincoln in 1996.

She described the celebration around the county courthouse, which included a huge silver arch over the road.

"This is small-town America at its best," she observed.

The State of Illinois recently became involved in Route 66 with the establishment of the Illinois Route 66 Heritage Project. Its mission is to increase tourism along Route 66, noting that, mile-for-mile, Illinois has more authentic Route 66 sites than any other state.

Tourism experts note that Route 66 is a perfect vacation for Baby Boomers, which is the largest and fastest-growing segment of the travel market.

"Not only are they the perfect age to get caught up in the '50s-'60s nostalgia of Route 66, the 66 travel experience offers many of the elements they are looking for," say project officials.

"As a 'create your own' travel experience trip, 66 addresses boomer needs for individualization and unique experience. With good, reasonable priced accommodations up and down the road throughout Illinois, they should find they quality they are looking for."

As a community, Lincoln is fortunate to have connections with two phases of American history, Route 66 and Abraham Lincoln sites. Let's appreciate the connection they give us to the past.

The Mother Road in Lincoln
February 12, 2005

Route 66. Just the name is magic. Michael Wallis

Lincoln's good fortune to be located along historic Route 66 brought it a measure of economic prosperity when the highway was a buzz of activity. The city is again capitalizing on its connection to this famous byway.

Next week the Lincoln/Logan Chamber of Commerce, the Economic Development Partnership and the Abraham Lincoln Tourism Bureau of Logan County move into their new offices on the corner of Route 66 and Fifth Street.

The building has been renovated with a retro 1950's décor. The facility has been dubbed the Information Station since tourists, community members and potential residents and business owners will be able to get answers to their questions about Logan County there.

The foyer will be open around the clock, with

maps and other visitor information available. The lobby will have Route 66 memorabilia on display, including a collection of Stetson China manufactured in Lincoln, loaned by Chamber Director Bobbi Abbott. A Sports Hall of Fame will feature Logan County athletes. Public restrooms will be available to travelers.

Phase two of the project will be renovating the exterior to resemble a Route 66 gas station. With architectural work for the façade nearly completed, chamber and tourism officials are looking to raise funds for construction.

A service station theme is appropriate for the building since a Shell station owned by Thomas Coady sat on that site during the Route 66 era.

Originally Route 66 ran through the heart of Lincoln. Signs designating that 1930-1940 route through town were installed a couple years ago. The Route 66 bypass around the city was marked years ago as part of the state's labeling of the famous road.

When Route 66 opened in the 1920's, Lincoln was the site of a big celebration which included aviators and a parade of marching policeman from Springfield. The new road, the first fully paved highway in Illinois, connected Lincoln with other communities such as Pontiac, Funks Grove, Springfield and Litchfield. It also placed the city on the highway that led to the great American West.

"Route 66 was almost like a big neighborhood," recalled Ivan Ray, who opened a DX service station in 1957 where the recently-closed Phillips 66 station stands at Fifth Street and Route 66.

"In its heyday, Route 66 was the only road from Chicago to LA," he said. "It connected people."

Like all service stations were at the time, Ray's business was full-service with attendants pumping gas and washing windows. Gas sold for 25 to 30 cents a gallon. A Coca-cola cost five cents.

With about 60 percent of his business from the Mother Road, Ray met interesting travelers from all over the country - from vacationers to migrant workers packed into pickup trucks.

"In the safe days of hitchhiking, people headed out West looking for a job or hoping to become a movie star," he said.

Ray himself traveled Route 66 from Oklahoma to Illinois when he was on leave while serving in the U.S. Army. He and his family later moved into a home along Route 66 where they lived for 30 years. During that time he and his wife Elaine became avid collectors of Route 66 memorabilia.

A few miles down the road from Ray's service station, at the corner of Route 66 and Woodlawn Road, was a Standard Oil station owned by brothers Norman and Wilfred Werth. They also operated the Silver Bell next door, which offered hot dogs, sandwiches, candy and ice cream.

Wilfred "Squeak" Werth built the 15-unit Redwood Motel in 1956 to serve Route 66 travelers. Many famous people who performed at the Logan County fairgrounds stayed there, including entertainers from the Lawrence Welk Show.

"It was a lot of work," Werth said of his time at the motel and service station, "but we loved every minute of it."

Werth drove the length of Route 66 twice, traveling

to Pasadena, California to visit his wife Dorothy's parents.

"In 1946 we left for California with our two kids and $157 in my pocket," he recalled.

Lincoln had numerous businesses along Route 66, but none was better known than the Tropics restaurant. The Mill, famous for its schnitzel, was another well known Route 66 restaurant. The Heritage House and Blu Inn also served hungry motorists and locals, along with the Tiz Rite truck stop, Midway Cafe and Quacker Box diner.

Chamber and tourist officials are optimistic about their more visible location on Route 66. They're hoping to get state signage directing people from Interstate 55 to their office, said Chamber President Patrick Doolin.

The facility will get lots of exposure this summer during the annual Route 66 drive sponsored by the Route 66 Association of Illinois. Motorists participating in the motor tour will drive through Lincoln on June 12. Numerous other Route 66 buffs, often from other countries, will see the information station as they travel the nostalgic route throughout the year.

Not only can residents reminisce about the bygone era of Route 66, they can celebrate its role in the city's future.

Preserving the Mill
July 26, 2006

Nostalgia's the most commercial commodity there is today; I believe it's true all over the world. Stan Kenton

A few years ago, Lincoln residents became enamored with the idea of building a giant Abraham Lincoln statue to attract tourists. They recognized the need for a major tourism draw.

Now Lincoln has the opportunity to create an important tourist attraction with much less effort - by preserving The Mill restaurant on old Route 66.

Although The Mill wouldn't have the notoriety of a huge Abe statue, as a Route 66 icon it would add another Logan County stop for motorists traveling the Mother Road.

Opened as the Blue Mill restaurant in 1929, the restaurant became well-known for its schnitzel after reopening as The Mill in 1945. It was popular among residents and visitors alike.

Currently The Mill is embroiled in a dispute between the City of Lincoln and the current owner who has been cited for violating city ordinance by allowing the rundown building to remain unsafe.

Earlier this month Logan County Associate Judge Don Behle ordered the owner to pay a $32,000 fine, $100 per day for the 322 days the building has been unsafe under his ownership. He plans to appeal the decision.

Recognizing The Mill's potential as a tourist site, the Abraham Lincoln Tourism Bureau of Logan County is working to save the building while staying out of the legal wrangling.

Restoration of The Mill would give Lincoln a truly accessible Route 66 landmark, noted Geoff Ladd, tourism bureau director. Historic tourism is Logan County's strong suit, he added.

"The only way to make historic tourism work is to preserve sites that might be a draw," he said. "Once they're gone, they're gone."

Ladd would like to see the former restaurant initially restored as a photo opportunity stop along Route 66.

Ideally, either the city or a nonprofit organization could take ownership of The Mill, he said.

The unsafe back section could be removed, with cosmetic repairs improving the appearance of the former restaurant. The hole in the roof could be fixed. The Mill lettering on the building could be straightened. The paddles on the windmill could be repaired. Landscaping could be added.

The uniqueness of the structure with the mechanized windmill makes it special, Ladd said.

"Up and down Route 66, buildings have been restored as photo ops," noted John Weiss, who spearheads preservation efforts for the Illinois Route 66 Association.

Weiss got a first-hand look at the structure recently with Ladd and Patty Ambrose, executive director of the Illinois Route 66 Heritage Project.

"It's one-of-a-kind, which is why it's worth saving," Weiss said. "The structure seems solid, but we don't know what's under the floor."

Once the legal complications are resolved, the state Route 66 association is willing to organize workdays to make The Mill structurally sound and attractive. Not only would the association bring in workers, they'd encourage interested residents to participate.

Among those who might want to help are customers of Hallie's on the Square. Owned by Brian Huffman - whose parents and grandparents operated The Mill - Hallie's restaurant serves The Mill's schnitzel.

Hallie's customers often reminisce about old times at The Mill, Huffman said. He has his own memories of the restaurant.

"Most people have two parents, but I felt like I had hundreds of parents with all the customers there," he recalled.

"I'd like to see it preserved," he said. "It saddens me to drive by it now."

Weiss' group has helped with numerous Route 66 projects. Restoration of the Standard Oil gas station in Odell — now the most photographed Route 66 spot in Illinois — has been its most ambitious undertaking. Association members also helped restore the Pig Hip Restaurant in Broadwell and move the Bunyon statue to

Atlanta.

"We don't try to save everything on Route 66," Weiss said. "That would be foolish. But The Mill is one of a kind, which is why it's worth saving.

Logan County is the only Illinois county with an entire contiguous stretch of Route 66, Ladd noted.

"It's hard to package The Mill or the Pig Hip as a travel destination, but it's easy to package Illinois Route 66 as an attraction," he said.

Since Lincoln doesn't have an accessible Route 66 attraction, it gets left out of Route 66 brochures and tours, and the city misses out on thousands of tourist dollars, he added.

If The Mill is restored, it could be used as a museum to attract even more people, he noted.

Ladd also has big ideas for other parts of Route 66 in Logan County. He'd like to see the old gas station in Elkhart restored and reopened. He'd also like to see the abandoned Ghost Bridge near the Lincoln Sportsman Club, west of the current Route 66 bridge over Salt Creek, accessible to the public. Even the Route 66-era motels like the Redwood could get new life with activity along the Mother Road.

New attractions could bring in more tourists and be an impetus for a new motel, which the city needs, Ladd said.

"If The Mill wasn't on Route 66, it wouldn't be worth our time," Ladd said.

(Editor's note: The Route 66 Heritage Foundation of Logan County was established in December, 2006 and now owns The Mill. They are in the process of turning it into a Route 66 photo attaction.)

The Lure of Route 66
July 1, 2006

Long ago, but not so very long ago, the world was different.
Lyrics from "Cars" soundtrack

It's easy to take our location along Route 66 for granted.

I was reminded of how special the Mother Road is when I saw the Disney Pixar animated movie "Cars" with my 10-year-old nephew recently.

Visiting from Houston, my nephew had no idea what Route 66 was until he saw the old highway featured prominently in the movie.

He isn't the only one. Youngsters and their parents — many of whom seldom read travel publications — are being exposed to the magic of Route 66.

The Disney movie tells the story of a race car stranded in the fictitious town of Radiator Springs, a sleepy community along Route 66. While there, he helps breathe new life into a town which shriveled up when bypassed by the interstate.

The film is a love letter to the heyday of the American road and the faded mystique of Route 66, one reviewer said. Another said it was filled with heartfelt nostalgia for the glory days of Route 66.

"'Cars' is introducing a whole new generation to the road," noted Patty Ambrose, executive director of the Illinois Route 66 Heritage Project.

Participants in a recent Route 66 conference in New Mexico reported the movie already is having an influence, she said. Youngsters are noticing landmarks along Route 66 they saw in the movie, she added.

"The movie is doing us a great service," echoed Marty Bilecki, public relations chairman for the Route 66 Association of Illinois. "It's telling the story of Route 66 — why the road was built, the type of people who drove the road and the creativity of people who created businesses and built their lives along the road."

"There's a big emphasis on getting the younger crowd involved in Route 66," noted Geoff Ladd, executive director of the Abraham Lincoln Tourism Bureau of Logan County. "The Illinois Route 66 Association is addressing that by offering free memberships to kids, which brings in soccer moms and dads."

Sally, a car in the movie, says, "Forty years ago, it wasn't about making great time, it was about having a great time," as she laments the fact the interstate now bypasses Radiator Springs.

"The road moved with the land; it didn't cut through it," she adds.

When Sally and the race car drive to a ridge where they can see how close-and yet how far-the interstate is from town, the race car exclaims, "They're just driving by! They don't know what they're missing!"

That comment could apply to Logan County as well, as motorists whiz by on I-55 unaware of the charming towns nearby.

"When they put in the interstate, it destroyed the infrastructure of rural America," observed Bilecki. "I saw a lot of destruction in Germany after World War ll. The destruction I saw in small towns along Route 66 on a recent trip reminded me of that."

The boom in tourism along the Mother Road, increasing with the release of "Cars," is helping turn that around.

"Route 66 already is bringing international visitors to Logan County," Ladd said. Travelers from other countries are driving the road in rental cars or in their own vehicles they've shipped here, he explained.

Ladd recently encountered French tourists at Horsefeathers gift shop in Elkhart. They couldn't speak any English, but they understood Route 66, he said.

A Japanese couple recently stopped at the county's information station, he said.

"They knew very few words in English, but they knew Route 66 and Abraham Lincoln," he added.

"Broadwell could easily be one of the smallest towns in the country with international visitors," he noted.

The number of international visitors no doubt will increase after the airing of a British documentary about the "Cars" movie filmed along Route 66.

"Scenes from our county will be viewed in England," Ladd said. "It's publicity you can't buy."

Communities along Route 66 need to be ready for the increase in visitors, Ambrose said. Her office has applied for grants to develop an interpretive plan to make the road a better experience for travelers.

The ultimate goal is economic development through tourism, allowing smaller communities to take advantage of being along a national scenic byway, she said.

Route 66 communities could take lessons from the fictitious Radiator Springs. The character Sally has local businesses ready to greet visitors, reminding them "It's a pleasure to take care of travelers on our road."

When lost motorists drive into town, she tells the business owners, "Customers are coming – you know what to do, just like we rehearsed."

"We are a town worth fixing up," she later tells the race car, adding, "one of these days we'll find a way to put it back on the map."

When Radiator Springs' main street is resurfaced, local shop owners realize they need to improve the appearance of their businesses as well.

In the end, the hero of the movie falls in love with the town. He helps restore it to its former glory by fixing the town's neon lights, patronizing local businesses and eventually moving his racing headquarters there.

Maybe the increase in tourism will bring similar benefits to Logan County.

"These are exciting times," Ladd said. "The movie just seals the deal."

"We couldn't have asked for a better thing to happen to the road," Ambrose echoed.

LJHS Building
July 12, 2003

The architectural profession gave the public 50 years of modern architecture and the public's response has been 10 years of the greatest wave of historical preservation in the history of man. George E. Hartman

The Lincoln Junior High School building, 78 years old, died this week from injuries inflicted by a demolition crew. Survivors include thousands of students who attended the school and hundreds of teachers employed there over the years.

As the wrecking ball plowed into the building, onlookers gathered to watch. Some were fascinated by the demolition efforts. Others saw the procedure as necessary to provide good schools for local students. Some couldn't even bring themselves to watch the destruction of such a beautiful historic building.

The older, ornate section of the building was built in 1925 as an addition to Lincoln High School, providing the students with a first-class gym. The $150,000 building also contained a chemistry lab, library and home economics and agriculture departments.

This school was one of the nation's many historic public schools built at a time when public education was revered. The public school was seen as a temple to democracy and learning, according to the National Trust for Historic Preservation. The phrases "to reveal truth and beauty" and "to develop intelligence and skill" engraved on the junior high building reflected that emphasis.

The building was among those solidly built with great craftsmanship and architectural distinction in that era. Not only was it the site where students' lives were enriched and they were equipped for the future, it also was the location for numerous sporting contests, proms and other memorable special events.

The 1925 building was remodeled after the high school moved to its new facility on Primm Road in 1959. It has served as Lincoln Junior High School since that time. In the 1960s the west addition replaced the 1899 original high school built on that site.

The demolition of the junior high building is part of an unfortunate nationwide trend of discarding handsome school buildings which once inspired civic pride, according to the National Trust. This is why the National Trust has placed historic neighborhood schools on its list of "America's 11 Most Endangered Historic Places."

Perhaps more than any other building type, historic neighborhood schools represent the bond between the community's past and present and the collective memory of thousands of local citizens, according to National

Trust officials. But across the country, thousands of these treasured landmarks have been reduced to rubble in recent years, they say.

LJHS is one of the most recent to "hear the sound of the school bell replaced by the crash of the wrecking ball." One reason the LJHS building met this fate was the result of state policies which favor new construction over renovation of existing schools.

Illinois is one of six states which offers financial incentives for local school districts to destroy existing buildings and construct new schools.

Both LJHS and Central School also faced the situation of being so neglected that demolition was preferred over renovation. "Deferred maintenance on existing schools can very well set the stage for unnecessary and costly expenses or demolition of historic schools," say National Trust officials.

"Sometimes the failure to properly maintain schools reflects the simple lack of funds for maintenance; often it reflects a deliberate strategy to let buildings deteriorate and then to use their deterioration as the justification for demolishing a school and replacing it with a new one," they explain.

"With the help of creative architects and sensible state policies, many school districts have demonstrated that historic schools can be brought up to 21st century standards and continue to serve the neighborhoods they anchored 50, 75 or even 100 years ago," National Trust officials pointed out.

It is unfortunate that in the debate over the future of Central and the Junior High, the assumption was made that only new schools could meet the needs of teachers and students when experience in other communities shows this is not necessarily the case.

"Building age is an amorphous concept and should not itself be used as an indicator of a facility's impact on student performance," according to Mark Schneider, an education expert at the State University of New York. "Many schools built as a civic monument in the 1920s and 1930s still provide, with some modernization, excellent learning environments; many newer schools built in the cost-conscious 1960s and 1970s do not."

Having been raised in the cities of Houston and Las Vegas, which pride themselves on tearing down the old to replace with the new, I missed out on the opportunity to enjoy historic buildings in my growing up years. Perhaps that explains my fondness for the many impressive historic buildings in Lincoln and my concern about their destruction.

Some of our historic buildings are important because they're beautiful and Lincoln would be less attractive without them. Others are worth saving because they have plenty of good use left in them. Some places are worth saving because they link us with our past and help us understand where we've come from and who we are.

That's what historic preservation is really all about, National Trust officials note. It's about hanging on to what's important. I'm saddened that these schools were not considered important enough to save.

Logan County Courthouse
November 5, 2005

A building has integrity just like a man. Ayn Rand

In 1905 Theodore Roosevelt was president, Albert Einstein published the theory of relativity and the First Russian Revolution broke out in St. Petersburg. That also was the year the current Logan County Courthouse was constructed in downtown Lincoln.

The building's 100-year history is being celebrated today with activities similar to those held for the 1905 building dedication. The festivities kick off with the "Looking Back, Moving Forward" parade downtown at 1 pm. Illinois Supreme Court Justice Rita Garman will speak at the 2:15 re-dedication ceremony in the third floor courtroom, followed by special music.

A reception and courthouse tours showcasing historical items on display will run from 3-5 pm. Main Street Lincoln's "Hats Off to Abe" auction of decorated stovepipe hats is scheduled for 5 pm.

The grandiose county courthouse is the heart of the county, with its central location within the county and its prominent spot on Lincoln's downtown square,

Not only is the building picturesque, it's been the focal point of various community activities over the years. Every Spring, high school students promenade down the courthouse steps during the Prom Grand March.

Until the recent computerization of election returns, the rotunda was a hotbed of activity on election night as residents gathered to watch election results posted by hand on a chalkboard.

For several years, dazzling Christmas trees brightened the first floor of the courthouse during the annual Festival of Trees.

Elected officer holders who work in the courthouse recognize what a treasure their workplace is.

"This building represents the rich history of Logan County," noted Circuit Clerk Carla Bender. "It's been the center of our community for 100 years. The outside is as majestic as it was 100 years ago."

"Anyone who works here appreciates the beauty of the courthouse," said County Treasurer Mary Ellen Bruns. "People who visit often comment on it."

"It's been an honor to work here," said Bruns, a 29-year employee of the Treasurer's Office.

Her office will be displaying the program from the 1905 courthouse dedication and an early photograph of the Board of Supervisors. One of Judge Lawrence Stringer's original books also will be displayed along with old treasurer's ledgers and an antique desk.

Very few 100-year-old courthouses are still in use, noted Circuit Judge David Coogan. Few have stained glass domes or large exterior clocks either, he added.

The third floor courtroom is the oldest circuit courtroom in continuous use in the state, Coogan noted. The 266-seat facility is much larger than most courtrooms.

The judge said the largest crowd he's seen in the courtroom was when 160 spectators came for the first day of a triple-murder trial in the 1970's.

The courtroom has numerous historical touches. Each wooden spectator chair has a metal hat rack underneath from the days when men wore hats regularly.

The oak counsel tables, jury box and judge's bench are all original as is the painting of three figures representing Mercy, Lady Law and Lady Justice.

The dumb waiter built to move documents from the circuit clerk's office on the second floor to the judge's office on the third floor is still in use.

The first floor courtroom was originally built as a meeting room for the Grand Army of the Republic, a Civil War veterans' organization, Coogan said.

"This building has served us well," he said. "It's a pleasure to work here although sometimes we take it for granted."

"When you walk in here, it feels like home," noted County Clerk Sally Litterly, who's worked in the building for 21 years. "The outside is beautifully unique. We need to preserve its historic value."

Numerous historic treasures have been discovered in the vault in her office. Litterly will be displaying the original drawing for the courthouse, an old plat book and a book of deeds from the county's 1839 founding.

A telegram from the governor directing county election officials to allow women to vote also will be displayed.

Lisa Madigan, daughter of the late Herman Dammerman who served as county treasurer for 26 years, has fond memories of the building from her childhood.

"I feel like I grew up in that building," she said. "We used to play in the courtroom when it wasn't being used. A big treat was when my dad would take us up to see the stained glass dome from the other side."

A stairway off the third floor leads to the area between the exterior dome and the interior stained glass dome.

"I don't have a childhood home to visit, but when I go into the courthouse I feel like I'm home," Madigan noted.

"The architectural features of the courthouse are outstanding," noted Former County Board Chairman Dick Hurley, who served many years as chairman of the county's Buildings and Grounds Committee.

"When you drive up I-55 or Highway 121, you can see the dome shining at night," he noted. The board paid to have the dome lit for that reason, he added.

"Even though the building looks strong, it's actually fragile," he said. "It needs regular maintenance. We spent a lot of money to keep it up, but you can't build that kind of building today.

"It's a building for the past, present and future," he added.

Community

Lincoln Experiences
March 19, 2005

The reality of any place is what its people remember of it.
                                           Charles Kuralt

As I read the "30 Things Every Midwesterner Should Experience" article in the March/April 2005 issue of Midwest Living magazine, I realized Lincoln has its own set of pleasures.

Midwest Living notes regional experiences are "woven so deeply into our proverbial fabric that we tend to take them for granted."

To paraphrase that article: "Behold, a wake-up call: Our list of essential Lincoln experiences. For nonresidents, they're clues that reveal who we are. For true-blooded Lincolnites, they're a gentle reminder."

Share in the excitement of a home Lincoln Community High School basketball game. Basketball is king in Lincoln, especially in years like this when LCHS earns a trip to the state tournament. Home games begin with starting players highlighted by a spotlight in a darkened gym while the pep band plays its pounding music and the crowd roars its enthusiastic approval.

In August, sense the magic of hot air ballooning as you stand alongside a brilliantly colored balloon while it's being inflated at the annual Lincoln Art and Balloon Festival. Seeing dozens of graceful balloons float overhead is a tranquil scene which lingers in your memory long after the festival.

Admire the speed and strength of contestants in the national railsplitting competition at the annual Abraham Lincoln National Railsplitting Festival. Seeing these men compete gives festivalgoers an appreciation for Abraham Lincoln's back-breaking work in his railsplitting days.

Delve into local Abraham Lincoln connections with a visit to the Lincoln College Museum and Postville Courthouse. See memorabilia from Abraham Lincoln's days in Logan County at the museum. Explore the replica of the rustic courthouse where Lincoln practiced law while traveling the Eighth judicial circuit.

Compare your hands and feet to Abraham Lincoln's. The lobby of State Bank of Lincoln at 111 N. Sangamon St. has molds of Lincoln's massive hands and feet to provide a literal hands-on experience.

Stand spellbound in the rotunda of the Logan County Courthouse, gazing up at the awe-inspiring stained glass dome. This year is an ideal time to visit this impressive historic building as the courthouse celebrates its 100th birthday.

Admire the glamorous dresses and sharp-looking tuxedos worn by high school students at the Grand March at the Logan County Courthouse. LCHS prom couples are announced to the crowd as they walk down the courthouse steps and along the sidewalks for friends and relatives to greet them.

Feast your eyes on the vivid autumn colors while strolling through Madigan State Park in the fall. Spotting a few head of deer can be an added bonus.

Let the twinkling white lights sprinkled throughout downtown mesmerize you while doing your holiday shopping in charming downtown Lincoln shops. The setting is reminiscent of a Norman Rockwell-style Christmas.

Feel the serenity of a snowfall blanketing historical homes on tree-lined streets. Neighborhoods are transformed into tranquil havens of powdery white in winter.

Breathe in the aroma of summer as you watch an exciting youth baseball game in the Lincoln Pony Baseball annual tournament. With the scent of fresh-mowed grass, hot dogs and leather gloves, you know it's summer.

Savor the refreshing tangy sweetness of a lemon shake-up at the Logan County Fair. This unique Midwestern beverage captures the essence of summer in one sip.

Linger over a tasty breakfast at Brandt's Arcade Café for a quintessential small town experience. The delicious food is matched by the scenic view of the Logan County Courthouse.

Taste the sweet, crunchy carmelcorn made onsite at Abe's Carmelcorn in downtown Lincoln. Although the shop offers other delectable specialty foods, none can top the mouth-watering carmelcorn.

Relax for a few minutes while reading a newspaper

or magazine in the delightful ambiance of the historic Lincoln Public Library, one of 105 Carnegie libraries in the state.

Immerse yourself in a delightful story acted out by local thespians at one of the Lincoln Community Theater summer productions. This year LCT is presenting "South Pacific", "I Hate Hamlet" and "Children of Eden."

Enjoy a Branson-style holiday extravaganza at the annual Christmas in the Chapel performances at Lincoln Christian College. The presentations feature impressive sets, costumes and musical talent of LCC students.

Revel in the excitement of the LCHS Homecoming Parade and the Christmas Parade. Hundreds of residents come out to wave at parade participants while children gather candy handed out along the route.

Appreciate the city's strong spiritual heritage by visiting one of the dozens of churches, many housed in stunning historic buildings. Purchasing delectable homemade food or unique handcrafted items at Lincoln Christian Church's huge Harvest of Talents is a great way to help raise money for world hunger relief.

Celebrate the city's ethnic diversity by attending the annual Martin Luther King service at Second Baptist Church. The speeches, the sermon and the music all are noteworthy.

These are among the memorable experiences in Lincoln. Let's not take them for granted

Bright Future Ahead
January 6, 2007

We are called to be architects of the future, not its victims.
R. Buckminster Fuller

Positive changes coming to Lincoln in 2007 and beyond are proof of the importance of planning for growth.

The west side of town will see more new businesses open this year. The new Super Wal-Mart, scheduled for completion this Spring, will be the largest. A Culver's restaurant will open just down the road and a new gas station is under construction near Cracker Barrel.

These kinds of developments don't happen in towns that are dying. Rather, they come to communities that choose to grow and seize the future.

With implementation of the Geographic Information System and a new regional comprehensive plan, the city and county are better prepared to grow, noted Rob Orr, executive director of the Lincoln and

Logan County Development Partnership.

"Having all the tools is huge," he said of the city's and county's ability to attract new businesses and residential developments.

"Our future is definitely brighter than it was with a plan from the 1970's," said Bill Glaze, chairman of the Regional Planning Commission, noting the new plan was worth the 18 months of preparation.

The commission will be working with planning professionals at the Tri-County Regional Planning Commission in Peoria to determine the best way to implement the new plan, Glaze said.

"We're moving forward, getting our ducks in a row," he said.

Several local non-government entities are setting a great example in how to plan for the future.

Lincoln College is finalizing its long-range planning effort, according to President John Hutchinson.

"Our new five-year plan will guide and direct our institution over the next several years," he said.

The college is moving forward very aggressively with its "If It Hadn't Been for Lincoln College" campaign designed to raise $7 million, he said.

The centerpiece will be the new Lincoln Center which will house an athletic/convocation facility and a greatly expanded college museum. Organizations in the community will be able to host athletic competitions and small conventions at the center. A fitness center open to the public also is planned.

"We hope to break ground in 2007," Hutchinson projected.

As part of the planning process, LC also has been

looking at community education in the Lincoln area, he said.

"We want to find out what people would like us to offer," he said, noting the college will be organizing a focus group to explore the issue.

As part of the planning process, LC officials also have decided to substantially revamp the entire admission process.

Most LC students currently come from Illinois, especially the Chicago area.

"We want to cast a wider net, into a five-state region, bringing geographic diversity to the college," he said. "We have a niche that attracts certain kinds of students."

Another entity seriously planning for its future is Abraham Lincoln Memorial Hospital, which recently announced its intent to move forward with plans for a new hospital on the westside of Lincoln to open in 2010.

The decision to build a replacement hospital evolved out of ALMH 2010, a 36-month research project to identify the best opportunities for providing excellent healthcare in Logan and eastern Mason counties. As part of the process, ALMH gathered input and direction from nearly 1,000 community members in surveys, focus group discussions and individual interviews.

Lincoln Christian College and Seminary also has focused on its future in developing the Lincoln 2015 campaign. The first phase is underway with renovation of the dining hall and construction of a three-story, 225-bed dormitory which will open next fall.

Acting on its vision "to become a national leader in Christian education," the school plans to hire an additional 16 faculty and 12 staff over the next nine years. A new seminary building also is planned.

"Opportunities for the future abound," noted President Keith Ray. "The time is right for us to embark on this unprecedented vision and plan. The best is yet to come."

LCCS Vice President of Stewardship Development Gary Edwards reflected on the importance of planning for the future.

"If organizations or institutions are going to grow, they need to prepare," he said. "Otherwise, you're playing catch up."

"The planning process is fun, but it can be frightening," he said. "You take reasonable risks as you plan for the future.

"You determine your strengths, your weaknesses and your opportunities, and decide how to play to your strengths and minimize your weaknesses.

"It's not a significantly different approach for the community," he noted. "But there's always a reluctance to make changes. We get very comfortable, but change takes us to a discomfort level.

"You have to decide if you want to be a pioneer or a settler. But if you settle down, the world passes you by and you die."

Historic Preservation
April 15, 2006

Any effort at revitalizing our downtown area must take root with the realization that it unquestionably must be done.

Alan Autry

Historic preservation is alive and well in Lincoln.

Recent renovation projects at two downtown businesses and two churches have enhanced the area's beauty.

The former J.C. Penney building on north Kickapoo Street is getting a new look. The unattractive aluminum covering the second story – probably put up during the 1970's "modern" era – was removed last year.

Restored windows were installed on the second floor this week, according to Tom O'Donohue, business manager for the family trust that owns the building.

The entrance has been moved back four feet and redone to expose the iron girder. A wall between the two front doors also has been removed. The new entryway is tiled with brick.

Additional improvements on the 100-year-old building include brick work, tuck pointing and acid washing of the capstones. The original tin ceilings also will be restored

O'Donohue plans to install an old-fashioned soda fountain, complete with a 1920's-era bobtail dispenser, this summer. The facility currently houses the Children of Pokot Educational Fund, which will remain there. O'Donohue lives upstairs, where he plans to add additional apartments.

"We've wanted to work on this building since we bought it," he said. "People are excited about what we're doing."

Around the corner on Broadway Street, Greg and Julie Tarter are making great strides in restoring the Hallmark store to its former beauty when it housed Landauer's Clothing Store.

When the Tarters purchased the business last summer, they renovated the back portion of the store. They removed the drop ceilings, restored the original tin ceilings and installed new carpet.

The wall which hid mirrors and cabinets used in Landauer's has been removed. Once again clothing is sold in the building, now that the Tarters have relocated That Place clothing shop from the building at the corner of Broadway and Kickapoo streets.

Working in stages, they're now redoing the front showcase windows at Hallmark. Beautiful wood paneling from the Landauer's days is visible again.

The original wooden Landauer's doors will be

installed and the front section of tin ceiling will be repaired.

This summer the Tarters plan to tackle the center section of the Hallmark store, removing the drop ceilings, repainting the original tin ceilings and laying new carpet.

The Tarters had already shown their interest in sprucing up historic buildings when they dressed up the corner spot where Glenn Brunk Stationers is now located by replacing an aluminum awning with an attractive canvas one on the first floor and repainting second-story awnings and window trim.

Greg and his employees at Tarter Brothers Mechanical have done most of the restoration work on the buildings.

A few blocks away, Zion Lutheran Church will be celebrating its first Easter with a new building addition that connects the 1903 sanctuary and the 1953 education building.

Church members recognized that existing buildings had physical limitations for members and guests, including numerous stairs and inaccessible restrooms.

They considered abandoning the downtown location and building a new church near Zion Lutheran School on Woodlawn Road. However, they decided to continue maintaining a downtown presence and be close to residential neighborhoods.

The new addition includes an elevator to both the sanctuary and the education building and new handicap accessible restrooms. A curbside drop-off area has been added and the church office now has easier access.

More classrooms for Bible studies and meetings,

as well as a larger space for fellowship before and after worship services, were added.

The architectural plan preserved the exterior historic appearance of the buildings while showcasing the attractive brick on the outer wall of the sanctuary which became an interior wall in the addition.

Members at Lincoln Christian Church at 204 N. McLean faced problems similar to Zion's, with an older sanctuary that had limited access and a need for more space. They also choose to connect their existing buildings, the 1954 sanctuary with its attached educational wing and the newer Fellowship Center.

Last year they added 20,000 sq. ft. of space, including a large area for fellowship between worship services they've named the Family Room. They installed an elevator to provide access to all levels and greatly expanded the space for their junior and senior high ministries. Additional meeting rooms were added and the church office was renovated.

"We discussed relocating to the edge of town with a modern building," noted Todd Parmenter, minister of administration. "Our decision to stay was based on the fact we are known as the downtown church. That is our heritage.

"The town is at the heart of our ministry, so we felt we needed to be in the heart of town," he explained.

Main Street Lincoln Director Wanda Lee Rohlfs is pleased to see historic preservation work taking place.

"Revitalization and restoration begats more revitalization and restoration," she observed. "When some property owners restore their property, those who haven't begin to realize they're out of sync, she explained.

Locally-Owned vs. Chain Stores
March 3, 2007

Know where to draw the line.
James P. Owen "Cowboy Ethics"

The opening of the Wal-Mart Supercenter next week will generate a lot of excitement. It's easy to become enamored with something new and large. Yet, let's not forget the locally-owned businesses which rely on our support.

One of the best is Lincoln IGA, with its reputation for quality, service and extremely generous support of community projects.

Hometown Proud - the slogan for the Independent Grocers Alliance — accurately reflects Lincoln IGA's approach to doing business.

"We believe a good grocery store isn't a sprawling, impersonal example of cookie cutter commerce, but a community hub owned and operated by the very people who know the area best — the citizens," says IGA Chairman

and CEO Dr. Thomas Haggai on the alliance website.
Lincoln IGA knows what its customers want.

"We're really well known for our freshly cut meat," noted Charlie Lee, who's owned IGA with Bill Campbell since 1990. "We cut it and grind it every day. You won't find that with some competitors whose meat might be cut in Nebraska or somewhere."

Lee also is proud of the store's fresh produce which is delivered four times a week. The deli also is known for its freshly prepared items.

"We sell more fried chicken than anybody, with four fryers going constantly," Lee said. "Our signature meat loaf is made in-house, and we bake our own breads and cinnamon rolls.

"It takes a lot of time and help," he said, noting other supermarkets are moving away from that kind of freshness. The store also carries IGA Brand products, a low cost alternative to national brands.

IGA's service also differentiates the store from its competitors. The store also has more checkers than their competitors, Lee said.

"We put people through quicker," he said. "No one likes to stand in line and wait. We get them out in a hurry."

Delivery of groceries to homebound customers is a unique IGA service. Orders are placed on Wednesdays and delivered on Thursdays.

"We started this during a snowstorm 15 years ago," said Campbell. "It's not profitable; it's a service."

IGA uses volunteer labor — Campbell's wife Ginny — to deliver groceries to the 30 customers who need it.

"She goes the extra mile, even shoveling the

sidewalk, or washing their hair," he added.

Special ordering is another service IGA offers, with customers often requesting specific products.

"We carry slow-moving items because people need them," Lee said. "We want to take care of our community."

"We carry more variety than any store in town," he added.

Small grocery stores were common in Lincoln years ago. In 1931, the city supported 44 grocers, Campbell said.

"We're fortunate to be the last one left," Lee said.

The Independent Grocers Alliance was formed to combat a threat similar to the one Wal-mart Supercenters pose today. In the 1920's, A & P stores initiated the spread of national grocery chains. IGA was formed in 1925 to unite independent grocers to help them compete.

"We're not a dying breed," Lee said. "We're changing with the times."

A fire seven years ago which gutted the store allowed Lee and Campbell to purchase all new equipment and become more efficient, which has held down costs.

When IGA rebuilt after the fire, Eaton/Cutler Hammer donated the power boxes and circuit breakers since the grocery store had done so much for the community over the years.

IGA added an additional 5,000 square feet two years ago, which Lee said put them in a position to be more competitive.

The store's location also works in its favor.

"We're where people live, and 1,200 people are employed within six blocks of the downtown square," Lee said.

"We've been fortunate," Lee said. "Business has been good. We reinvest in the community.

"With all the business our customers give us, we want to support their ball teams, their causes, their fundraisers," he added.

"If Wal-Mart gave as much as we have, they'd have to spend $10 million in our community," Campbell noted, adding that he's read that Wal-Mart's strategy is to run off local businesses.

"If customers don't shop here, we can't stay open," he said. "We offer a great product at a good price with lots of service."

An investigation by a comparison-shopping Web site, "The Grocery Advantage," questions how much consumers really save at Wal-Mart.

"That's got to be one of the biggest misperceptions out there, that Wal-Mart has everyday low prices," said grocery analyst Michael Berberick of "The Grocery Advantage".

After analyzing thousands of weekly grocery prices in three cities for nearly a year, he discovered that with smart shopping, customers can save more at traditional grocery stores than at Wal-Mart. Customers can find better deals in the weekly ads, he said.

"Wal-Mart has no items on sale. They only have an everyday low price," Berberick said.

Wal-Mart won't double your coupons, as most traditional stores do, he added.

So, after visiting the new Lincoln Wal-Mart Supercenter, let's not forget what IGA and other locally-owned businesses provide.

What Newcomers Enjoy
December 2, 2006

It was a marvelous advantage to grow up in a small town where you knew everybody. Warren Christopher

What do you like about living in Lincoln?

Small-town life and proximity to surrounding cities are what appeal to newcomers, according to local real estate brokers.

New residents like the small-town friendliness compared to places like Springfield where you might not even meet your neighbors, noted Linda Barrick of ME Realty. Everyone talks about strangers here waving to them like they've known them for years. she added.

Becky Werth of Werth and Associates has found potential residents like the friendliness, too.

"In a large community, you might find that in a neighborhood, but not throughout town," she said.

Potential residents also mention the friendliness in the downtown stores, Barrick said.

"A lot of people tell me how impressed they are with our downtown, when so many downtowns have gone by the wayside as malls came along," she added.

Werth's clients have noticed how vibrant and alive the downtown district looks also.

"I hear a lot of comments about how beautiful the downtown looks," echoed David Alexander of Alexander and Company Real Estate. "Newcomers think it's quaint."

"People consider Lincoln a nice place to go to church and to get involved," he added.

They like the charm of the community, including streets with beautiful older homes, Werth said.

Greg Brinner of RE/MAX Hometown Realty has also heard comments on the well-kept older homes and the brick streets.

"We might not have everything, but if we don't it's only 30 to 40 miles away," Werth pointed out. "It the best of both worlds to take advantage of big city opportunities while having the benefits of a community that cares about people."

The convenience of commuting to surrounding cities — especially when spouses work in different cities - brings new residents to town.

"We have easy access to the interstate and it's a short commute," Werth said.

The opening of 155 between Lincoln and Peoria has brought people to Lincoln who have a spouse working in Peoria, in addition to those with spouses working in other nearby cities, Brinner said.

Bob Albert of Albert Realtors has found his clients like Lincoln's geographic location, with five large cities within an hour's drive.

His clients also are impressed with the Recreation Center and all it offers.

Werth also has noticed new residents appreciate the Rec.

"It's a phenomenal facility for a community this size," she said.

"We also get questions about our schools," Werth said. "They like the fact that the schools here don't have to be police patrolled."

Brinner's clients appreciate the low crime rate.

The real estate market in Lincoln has always been fairly stable, Alexander said.

'We've never had any really high highs or any really low lows," he said. "With factories and farming, we've never had a serious downturn – not even when LDC closed."

Lincoln hasn't had a real estate bubble like the East and West Coasts, Brinner noted.

"I've had a better year this year than last, and last year was a record-setting year," he said.

"Our per-square-foot prices here are better than in Bloomington or Springfield," Alexander pointed out. "And the average house sale in Lincoln is $80,000 while in Springfield, it's $100,000."

Alexander is optimistic about Lincoln's future.

"We're turning the corner with Robert's Sysco, the ethanol plant and the Super Wal-Mart," he said. "For the first time in a long time, the attitude is positive."

"We're finally starting to leverage our central location which I've heard about since I was a kid," he said.

Barrick said that for years her father-in-law talked about how Lincoln's central location is like the hub of a wheel.

Lincoln is slowly growing, but a new subdivision would help a lot, Brinner said.

Buyers are looking for homes with larger rooms to accommodate the new popular oversized furniture, he said. New medium-priced homes, which would provide those, are the key to residential growth in the city, he added.

"We probably need another subdivision," Werth agreed. "We need new three-bedroom, two-bath ranch style homes, the typical property Mr. and Mrs. Average American look for."

"A lot of people in management want new homes," Barrick added.

The realtors all agree any new subdivisions should be quality developments and not inexpensive, cheaply built homes.

With prices so high, it's hard for contractors to build on speculation, Albert pointed out.

He also noted a lot of buyers would like to rent first, but three- or four-bedroom rental homes are about impossible to find.

Once newcomers find housing, they're excited about living here.

Fairs and Festivals
August 17, 2002

The only real action takes place on the bridge between people. Anonymous

Technology has greatly impacted our lives. Its marvels are incredible and its conviences enticing.

Yet obsession with technology can leave us isolated and withdrawn from human interaction.

Fortunately here in Central Illinois we have an antidote to the malady — an abundance of fairs and festivals with lots of opportunities for human connection.

"America is the most technologically advanced country in the world," writes social forecaster John Naisbitt in his latest book, "High Tech/High Touch: Technology and Our Accelerated Search for Meaning."

"Softened by the comforts technology brings to our lives, fascinated by its gadgetry, reliant on its constant companionship, addicted to its steady delivery of entertainmen . . . Americans are intoxicated by technology."

Symptoms of technological isolation include "blurring the distinction between real and fake" and "living our lives distanced and distracted" Naisbitt says.

Social interaction at fairs and festivals counteracts these trends. Instead of watching actors exchange dialog on the TV show "Friends," fairgoers can have conversation with real-life friends.

Rather than passively viewing life on TV, folks at festivals have first-hand experiences, such as standing next to a hot air balloon as it's being inflated and being surrounded by the deafening roar of a tractor pull competition.

Socializing has always been a big appeal of fairs and festivals. Our busy lifestyles prevent us from visiting with friends and acquaintances as much as we'd like. But festivals provide time for leisurely chats rather than brief greetings at the supermarket or church.

When we moved to Lincoln from California 11 years ago, we were amazed at the fairs and festivals in the area.

We arrived shortly before the Logan County Fair. We took in the sights there and traveled to the Illinois State Fair a few days later.

Then the Lincoln Art and Balloon Festival captivated us. We journeyed to Atlanta and Mt. Pulaski for their fall festivals and attended the National Railsplitting Festival here in Lincoln.

A trip to the Apple and Pork Festival in Clinton rounded out our special event spree that year.

We were thrilled with our introduction to life in the Midwest through these events. Our experiences epitomized what we hoped to discover in relocating to this part of the country.

Our children, ages 6, 3 and 8 months at the time, were fascinated by buildings full of cattle, sheep and hogs - all close enough to touch — at the county and state fairs.

The midway exhibits provided a glimpse into Midwestern life. Delicious lemon shake-ups - unheard of in California - introduced us to the many new tastes we were to encounter in the Midwest.

Cultural identity is one reason fairs and festivals are so popular. They showcase local people and communities to newcomers. They promote civic pride as they convey "this is who we are."

For long-time residents, attending fairs and festivals is a tradition with unforgettable memories. County fairs have been times for showcasing livestock, impressive garden produce, fine artwork and top-quality home-baked items.

Food is another appeal of fairs and festivals. Corn dogs and Culler's fries beckon county fair attendees. Walleye sandwiches entice balloon festival visitors. Kettle corn is a favorite at the railsplitting festival.

But fairs and festivals have another important aspect — they contribute to the local economy and raise funds for sponsoring organizations.

The art and balloon festival attracts 20,000 to 30,000 people every summer. Motels are filled to capacity. Visitors also patronize other businesses, from gas stations to restaurants to specialty shops.

The Lincoln/Logan Chamber of Commerce has even capitalized on the event to woo corporate folks with special VIP tents at the fairgrounds.

An outstanding and unique event, the art and balloon festival enhances community pride. Few remain unmoved by the sight of dozens of brightly colored balloons lifting off at the festival. A beautiful downtown park brimming with artists' booths is a shopper's dream.

In addition to providing a memorable event, the balloon fest also generates funds for the chamber.

Local organizations have the opportunity to raise money at the festival by operating a food booth or activities such as the YMCA Children's Art Tent.

Later in the year, the Festival of Trees in the Logan County Courthouse attracts 3,000 people to downtown Lincoln during the holiday shopping season.

A popular holiday tradition for residents, the event also raises money for its organizers, the Abraham Lincoln Healthcare Foundation and Main Street Lincoln.

Next weekend, whether you want to experience the thrill of watching hot-air balloons fill the sky, indulge in delectable food, visit with friends or help local organizations, shut down your computer and turn off your DVD player and head out to the balloon festival.

Funeral Visitations
June 22, 2002

Friends multiply joys and divide griefs. J.G. Bohn

The funeral home was packed. People of all ages waited in line for two-and-a-half hours.

As I attended the funeral visitation this week for Andy Pettijohn, the young businessman who died in a car accident, I reflected on this Midwest tradition of funeral visitations.

When we moved to Lincoln, I had to adjust to a new way of comforting grieving families. In the South and out West where I've lived, people don't have official visitations at funeral homes. Close friends and family members gather at the home of the deceased when word comes of death, just as they do here.

But in other parts of the country, only a few folks stop by the funeral home since there might not be any family members there. Those who want to express condolences either mail a card, send flowers, make a memorial donation or attend the funeral. None of those options provide for direct interaction with family members, however.

At first, funeral visitations struck me as an event which put the family through unnecessary trial. They seemed an invasion of privacy during such a personal time.

But I observed that the show of support evident at funeral visitations was appreciated by the family.

Yes, it was sad - maybe even gut-wrenching - for family members to talk with person after person at the visitation. But the shared memories, the retelling of funny or heartwarming stories, the promises of prayers all seem to provide needed support and help healing begin.

Sure, nothing will bring back a husband and father. But seeing hundreds of people waiting in line is quite a tribute to a loved one who has died. In an age where most folks are extremely busy, being willing to wait in line for two-and-a-half hours is quite a statement.

Some of those waiting have bad knees, or are on oxygen, or are pregnant. Standing for long periods of time isn't comfortable for them, but they do it.

With no prior experience with visitations, one thing I had to figure out was what to say to the family. We all want to say something appropriate.

According to the etiquette books, merely saying "I'm sorry" is sufficient. Just the person's presence at the visitation expresses a lot.

Seeing the body in the casket also was an adjustment for me at visitations. Most funerals I attended prior to moving to Lincoln either had a closed casket or were memorial services held after the burial.

I remember the first funeral I attended in Lincoln.

When I walked into the small narthex of the church, I turned around after signing the guest book and was face-to-face with the body in the open casket. It was quite disconcerting, to say the least.

Over the years, I've changed my opinion about viewing the body. At first it seemed morbid and unnecessary. Now I see how viewing the body of the deceased helps bring closure in the grieving process. It also presents death as part of life, rather than something hidden away.

Interestingly enough, this decades-old tradition of funeral visitations is in keeping with a new trend of making the grieving process more personal. As hospice programs have changed the way many people deal with dying nationwide, people want a more personal experience with grieving. The Midwest has been doing that for years.

Part of that trend, apparent at visitations here in Lincoln, is displaying photographs of the loved one along with special mementos. Andy Pettijohn's visitation, for instance, had posters of hot air balloons.

Also gaining popularity is the practice of having people write down memories of the deceased. This idea was especially touching at Andy's visitation where the written recollections will be put into a book for Andy's young children.

"We've gone to where death is coming out of the closet," Psychologist Tom Bruce said in a news report in funerals in the Sacramento Bee. Bruce teaches a death and dying at Sacramento (CA) City College.

"The song may be over, but it was a wonderful song," he said. "We're sad, but we're celebrating. In their tears, they're finding warmth, they're finding laughter. That seems to me to be optimally healing."

It sounds like optimal healing is facilitated by the funeral visitations the Midwest has been doing all along.

Christmas Parade
November 26, 2005

Everyone loves a parade. Anonymous

Constructing a parade float and organizing the youngsters riding on it can be a chaotic experience. But seeing the delight on the little ones' faces made it worth the effort when I organized a Girl Scout float in the Lincoln Christmas Parade a decade ago.

That same motivation to enthrall parade participants and spectators must be what keeps the Lincoln Christmas Parade from suffering the fate of parades in other American towns.

"The hometown parade is disappearing," claimed the Wall Street Journal in its Oct. 29, 2005 article "The Passing Parade." With costs up and crowds down, cities across the country are seeing a decline in this American tradition, according to the WSJ.

The International Fairs and Festivals Association estimates there are 1,600 community parades annually.

At least 90 smaller-sized parades have folded in the past five years, association officials say.

Lincoln residents are fortunate the trend hasn't struck here. Sponsored by the Lincoln/Logan Chamber of Commerce and the City of Lincoln, the Lincoln Christmas Parade regularly has 100 or so entries. The 2005 parade, with the theme "Christmas in Motion Pictures," begins downtown next Thursday at 6:30 pm.

The waning of community parades "marks the decline of a time-honored Main Street ritual that allowed civic groups from the Boy Scouts to the Shriners to express local pride and promote themselves," the WSJ said.

Lincoln has kept this memorable tradition alive, which gives businesses and organizations the opportunity to express their civic pride and promote themselves. There's not even an entry fee.

The prize categories reflect the variety of entries. First, second and third place winners are selected in the business/industry/government category, the religious/youth/charitable category and the not-for-profit category.

The parade's grand prize winner, selected by community judges, gets $100. Winners of the Mayor's Award, the Chamber Award and the Grand Marshall's Award each receive $50.

"We haven't seen a decline or disinterest in the parade at all," noted Bobbi Abbott, chamber executive director. "The parade provides good exposure for businesses and groups. A lot of the success has been CITV 5's coverage. They broadcast the parade over and over."

The chamber has developed Ho-Ho-Holiday Coupons to help chamber members promote their businesses to the hundreds of parade-goers. The coupons, available only at the parade, contain discount offers from participating firms.

"Several coupon sponsors saw quite a return by participating," Abbott said. "They said it was probably the most successful promotion they've done, in terms of getting customers into their stores."

Not only does the parade provide exposure for local firms and organizations, it's a lot of fun.

Girl Scout Troop 53 members are dressing up with antlers this year to portray the movie "Rudolph," tying in with the parade's motion picture theme. The girls will be on a flat bed trailer with a house, a sleigh, artificial snow and lots of lights.

"We have almost 100 percent participation from the girls," noted co-leader Shelly Jones. "They like being in the limelight and seeing their friends when they go around."

"For the size town it is, Lincoln has a big parade," she said. "When we moved here two years ago, it blew my mind."

High school students with the 4-H Federation are decorating a float based on the movie "National Lampoon's Christmas Vacation," noted Amy Hyde, 4-H Youth Developer.

"It'll have a house on a rack wagon with lots of Christmas lawn ornaments. The kids are excited."

Nobbe Eye Care Center will showcase its business with its "For Your Eyes Only" entry, featuring Dr. Todd Nobbe as James Bond and his staff in eyeball costumes.

"We love Christmas," Nobbe said. "In the parade, the community gets a chance to see you. We have fun."

U.S. Marines will be marching in the parade representing the Marine Corp Reserve's Toys for Tots. Spectators are encouraged to bring new, unwrapped toys to the parade to donate. All toys collected in Logan County stay in the county.

No parade is complete without bands. The Lincoln Community High School band and the Lincoln Junior High School band are regular participants. Other school bands join them when possible.

Also in the parade will be Chamber President Patrick Doolin as grand marshal. In keeping with tradition, the grand finale will be the arrival of Santa Claus, courtesy of the Lincoln Elks Club.

The parade is so popular, the Oasis Senior Center has piggybacked on the event for its biggest fundraiser of the year, a chili supper which runs from 3-7 pm. Last year more than 500 people took advantage of the convenient downtown location and delicious meal. CEFCU is the business sponsor of the event.

The Oasis also stays open after the parade for children to tell Santa Claus what they want for Christmas. The youngsters, who receive a special gift from the Oasis, also can have their photo taken with Santa for $3.

The Christmas Parade couldn't run smoothly without volunteer help. Chamber Member Diane Slack and her crew makes sure participants line up correctly and that there are no Santas other than the official one. Using radios loaned by the Logan County Emergency Management Agency, they try to avoid gaps.

"It's neat to see the community come together in the cold weather," Slack said. "I love Christmas."

The Lincoln City Hall anchors this corner of the 14-block Courthouse Square Historic District.

Zion Lutheran Church is one of many historic churches in Lincoln.

The Logan County Courthouse is visible throughout downtown, including nearby Scully Park. *Photo courtesy of Main Street Lincoln*

Lincoln College was dedicated to Abraham Lincoln on Feb. 12, 1865, the president's last living birthday. The cornerstone for University Hall (shown here) was laid a few months later.

Abraham Lincoln's influence is seen everywhere including this unique wall mural downtown.

The "Lincoln the Student" statue sits outside the Lincoln College Museum.

The "Divine Servant" statue of Jesus washing his disciple's feet reflects the attitude of servanthood emphasized at Lincoln Christian College.

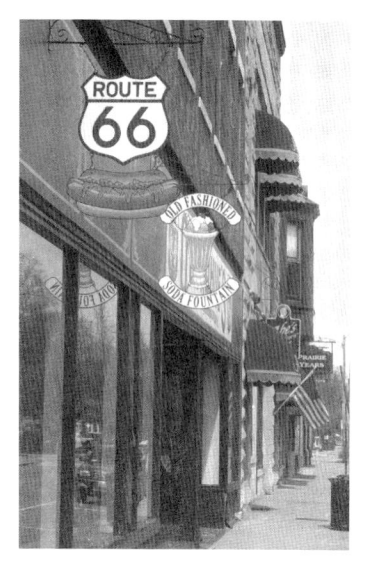

A variety of popular speciality shops and restaurants are located in downtown Lincoln's Courthouse Square Historic District.

The Tropics, a popular restaurant and Route 66 icon, sits idle for now.

The Lincoln Public Library is proud of its heritage as a Carnegie Library.

Lincoln Community High School, home of the Railsplitters, is known for its successful basketball and speech teams.

The Lincoln Art and Balloon Festival is a highlight of the year for residents and visitors alike. *Photo by Kent Hower, courtesy of Lincoln Logan Chamber of Commerce*

Estate Auctions
July 8, 2006

If we ever take the theater out of the auction business, it would be an awfully boring world. A. Alfred Taubman

Despite having lived in several different states, until I came to the Midwest I'd never seen an estate sale.

When my widowed grandmother became too ill to live in her Louisiana home, her possessions were divided among family members with leftovers given to charity. That's standard procedure in many states.

Estate sales are common in the Heartland, however. They follow the long-standing practice of selling farm animals (and later machinery) along with farmland at auctions, according to auctioneer Mike Maske. These auctions evolved to include household items and even houses.

Although auctions are one of the oldest methods of sale around, they continue to thrive and are popular with both buyers and sellers, according to the National

Auctioneers Association.

Auctioneers create a competitive and entertaining atmosphere which attracts consumers to the sale, NAA officials note. Their hand gestures, eye contact with the crowd and rhythmic chant stirs buyers and brings the sale to life. It's what separates auctions from other types of sales.

"Sellers get quick turnaround for their merchandise at fair market value while buyers can find unique items and bid at prices they can afford," said NAA president Dennis Kruse.

When people move out of their homes, they can't keep everything, Maske said. Auctioneers market those items for their customers.

Advertising is a key part of that process.

"You can't sell to empty seats," he said. "You have to know where to send the sale bill and who to talk to. A week or two before a sale, I'll call collectors and remind them."

Auctions attract several kinds of buyers, he noted. Some buy for resale, others for a personal collection. Young couples buy furniture for their homes.

Many buyers purchase items as a keepsake to remember a friend or relative, he said, noting sentimentality is a real seller.

The Internet is starting to impact local auctions. Some customers buy items to sell on Ebay.

"It's another extension of our market," Maske said, "It allows us to sell to people on the East or West Coast who would never come to the sale."

The recent Carl Ebberstein estate auction in Cornland, with an extensive collection of antique tractors, used an Internet auction system, Maske said. People viewed photographs of the tractors and placed bids online until two days before the auction, he explained. During the live auction, potential buyers could hear the bidding via a direct feed and could place bids online, he said.

Col. Dan White and his wife Pam have used the Internet to send photos of collectibles to potential buyers, such as the sugar shakers recently sold to an Iowa resident.

The couple uses a building they purchased in 2004 - dubbed The White House — for many of their auctions.

The Whites take pride in the fact they present a clean sale, washing all household items and placing them on white sheets, rather than in boxes.

"We treat everyone's belongings with respect, as if it were ours," White said.

If a couple moves out of their home, the Whites can handle the sale from start to finish. Not only will they clean and inventory items in the home, they'll make sure the house gets cleaned and even auction it off if the owners desire.

"We've sold houses from $20,000 to $180,000," White said.

White has been an auctioneer for 20 years, adopting the optional colonel auctioneer title which goes back to Civil War days when colonels sold land to the soldiers.

In addition to the auction business, the Whites farm 1,000 acres

Maske, trained as an auctioneer 30 years ago, fell in love with auctions when regularly visiting the Clinton Livestock Show as a kindergartener. He's currently certified by the Auction Marketing Institute.

In addition to auctioneering, Maske serves as secretary of the Logan County Fair Board.

At auctions, Maske focuses on moving items as quickly as possible, selling 100-125 items an hour.

"It's not how fast you talk, it's how many items you sell," he explained. "If you start at 10 am, you'd better have the good stuff sold by 2 pm."

"The chant is so important," he noted. "It encourages people to bid. If it's too fast for an audience, they won't bid."

Both Maske and White use ringmen to roam the floor, answering bidders' questions and displaying items as they're auctioned.

Popularity of auction items varies. Antiques in good condition sell well, as does glassware and other collectibles. Arrowheads are especially hot now.

Many auction attendees find the experience addictive, NAA officials claim. They say there's nothing quite like the thrill of finding something you want and then bidding against others who want the same thing.

You don't have to be a seasoned auction attendee to experience the thrill of auctions. Auctioneers are glad to welcome new bidders.

Although almost everyone has heard the story about the person who attended an auction, scratched his nose and came home with an item he didn't intend to buy, pay no heed to that myth, NAA officials say.

"People who've never been to an auction certainly should give it a try," said John Roebuck, an NAA official. "Don't be intimidated - go and have fun!"

Lincoln Sesquicentennial
September 6, 2003

The song is ended, but the melody lives on. Irving Berlin

Music always enhances celebrations. The Lincoln Sesquicentennial was no exception.

Music was featured in many of the festivities, from the American English rock group to the 33rd Illinois Volunteer Regiment Band.

Yet some of the most memorable music was that performed by local amateur crooners. Curtis Sutterfield delivered an outstanding version of the national anthem and "God Bless America" at the Sesquicentennial opening ceremony. Don Ludwig, too, did an exceptional job singing the national anthem both nights of the Lincoln Art and Balloon Festival.

Another terrific vocal performance was Doug Rohrer's rendition of the official state song, "Illinois," with the Illinois Symphony Orchestra at the Sesquicentennial closing concert.

"Illinois" was included in the Lincoln concert at

the request of Mayor Beth Davis. "Ever since hearing 'Illinois' sung at my graduation from the University of Illinois at Springfield years ago, I've loved that song," the mayor explained. "I knew it would be appropriate at the Sesquicentennial."

Rohrer, son of Mike and Darla Rohrer, volunteered to sing the piece when he learned of Davis' interest in it. A Lincoln Community High School senior who's performed in numerous musical productions, he was a natural.

He was able to obtain the music from his vocal instructor, Linda Buffington. After practicing a few times, he auditioned for Davis. She was so pleased with how he sang it, she contacted the symphony orchestra which was scheduled to perform at the Sesquicentennial. Orchestra Conductor Karen Lynne Deal thought including the song was a great idea even though the orchestra had never played it before.

Rohrer sent Deal the music to "Illinois," which had to be arranged into a score for an orchestra performance. Meanwhile, he continued to refine his rendition of it. He was able to practice it only once with the orchestra before the Sesquicentennial concert.

Singing the song at the concert was a great experience, Rohrer said. "I tried not to be nervous. But it was a completely different situation than I usually perform in, so it was totally nerve-wracking," he admitted, although his polished presentation gave no hint of any jitters.

Rohrer's performance was well received by the audience. "It meant a lot to people to have 'Illinois' as part of the Sesquicentennial," he said. "They also liked seeing what someone from Lincoln could do with it."

"He did an absolutely wonderful job," noted Davis. "I had tears coming out of my eyes."

Deal echoed the mayor's comments. "Doug moved me with his performance. I thought it was beautiful."

For many in the audience, it was the first time they'd heard the state song. Written in the mid-1800's with music by Archibald Johnston and lyrics by Charles H. Chamberlain, "Illinois" served as the state's unofficial song for many years before the 54th General Assembly passed a bill making it official.

Some might have recognized the melody from hearing the Marching Illini Band at the University of Illinois play it during their pre-game shows in the 1950s. Not only is Davis a fan of the song, others have come to appreciate it. Rohrer admitted at first he wasn't that crazy about the song. "After hearing it with the full orchestra, you get to love it," he said.

Deal liked the song, too. "I think the melody is gorgeous and the words are very touching," she said. "I would love to do it again and it would be great to do it with Doug should the opportunity arise. He is such a nice young man. I was so proud of him."

In the meantime, since most of us are unfamiliar with the lyrics, they're printed below. Those who have RealAudio or MP3 can listen to the song being sung at the Illinois History Resource Page, www.historyillinois.org/hist.html.

By thy rivers gently flowing, Illinois, Illinois,
O'er thy prairies verdant growing, Illinois, Illinois,
Comes an echo on the breeze.
Rustling through the leafy trees, and its mellow tones are these, Illinois, Illinois,

And its mellow tones are these, Illinois.
From a wilderness of prairies, Illinois, Illinois,
Straight thy way and never varies, Illinois, Illinois,
Till upon the inland sea,
Stands thy great commercial tree, turning all the world to thee, Illinois, Illinois,
Turning all the world to thee, Illinois.
When you heard your country calling, Illinois, Illinois,
Where the shot and shell were falling, Illinois, Illinois,
When the Southern host withdrew,
Pitting Gray against the Blue, There were none more brave than you, Illinois, Illinois,
There were none more brave than you, Illinois.
Not without thy wondrous story, Illinois, Illinois,
Can be writ the nation's glory, Illinois, Illinois,
On the record of thy years,
Abraham Lincoln's name appears, Grant and Logan, and our tears, Illinois, Illinois,
Grant and Logan, and our tears, Illinois.

Being Connected
November 13, 2004

To know another, and to be known by another – that is everything. Florida Scott-Maxwell

As sirens blared and car horns honked around town last Saturday night, residents looked out their windows to determine the cause of the commotion.

The racket was the sound of families escorting the Lincoln Community High School band into town as it returned home from its first-ever appearance at the national Bands of America competition in Indianapolis.

Upon arrival at the school, LCHS Band Director David Swaar was greeted with thunderous applause. He basked in the glow of the moment while delivering an impromptu speech praising band students and thanking families for their support.

The scene could have been lifted from a heartwarming movie, with the soundtrack swelling with dramatic, uplifting music.

Incidents like this show Lincoln at its best. In a society plagued by citizens in isolation, Lincoln and other small towns can be places where residents feel more connected.

As I looked around at a roomful of strangers while dining at a Springfield restaurant recently, I realized I'd become accustomed to seeing familiar faces when eating out. Greeting other diners is half the fun of eating at Guzzardo's, Brandt's Arcade Cafe, First Wok, Blue Dog Inn, McCarty's at the Depot, Einstein's Louisiana Coffeehouse and other local restaurants.

The Zonta Turkey Dinner last Sunday was a perfect opportunity to see friends while enjoying a delicious meal. In addition to supporting a worthwhile organization, it's great to touch base with people I don't see often.

Shopping in Lincoln's charming downtown specialty shops is far more enjoyable than traipsing through a large, nondescript shopping mall. The merchandise is unique. Clerks are more helpful and other shoppers friendlier. As an added benefit, customers also know their sales tax dollars are benefiting their own community.

Main Street Lincoln's Home for the Holidays celebration last weekend offered entertainment, carriage rides and delicious goodies to enhance the downtown shopping experience.

The Lincoln/Logan Chamber of Commerce is in the midst of its Trade Inside the Box campaign, a series of promotions to encourage customers to shop locally.

Ho-Ho-Holiday Shopping Coupons will be handed out at the Christmas Parade as the newest promotion. Not only will residents have the opportunity to mingle with each other and celebrate the season when attending the parade, they'll also receive discount coupons from more than 20 local businesses.

Local residents need these opportunities to connect with each other.

In his best-selling book "Bowling Alone: The Collapse and Revival of American Community," author Robert Putnam relates how Americans have become increasingly disconnected from family, friends and neighbors.

Putnam draws on research to show that Americans belong to fewer organizations, know their neighbors less, meet with friends less frequently and socialize less with their families than they did 40 years ago. They're even bowling alone rather than in leagues.

Family structure, suburban life, changes in work, television, computers and women's roles have contributed to this decline, Putnam says.

His follow-up book, "Better Together: Restoring the American Community," Putnam describes how Americans are developing new ways of making connections among people. They're reestablishing bonds of trust and understanding and revitalizing civic spirit, he says.

Putnam encourages people to build social networking by creating new ties and strengthening old ones. He suggests numerous ways to do this, including supporting local merchants, attending school plays and joining the local Elks, Kiwanis or Knights of Columbus.

He also recommends attending home parties when invited and hosting a block party or open house. He suggests giving to the food pantry, seeing if your neighbor needs anything when you run to the store and offering to rake the neighbor's yard.

He says to turn off the TV and talk with friends or family or collect oral histories from older town residents.

Eating breakfast at a local gathering spot on Saturdays is another recommendation, which ties in with concepts promoted by Ray Oldenburg in "The Great, Good Place."

Places where citizens meet to develop friendships, discuss issues and interact with others have always been important to communities, Oldenburg says. He calls these locations "third places," with home being the first place and work the second.

These third places make people feel at home and create a sense of community. They provide companionship and encourage sociability instead of isolation.

Third places must be free or inexpensive to enter and to purchase food and drink. They should be easily accessible so people make the place a regular part of their routines. People should be welcome there and find it easy to enter conversation.

Lincoln is among the Main Street communities promoting such places. A recent National Main Street Trends survey shows many Main Street towns are reporting an increase in restaurants, especially those described as "community gathering places."

Hopefully over the holidays Lincoln residents will take advantage of opportunities to connect with each other whenever possible.

Picturesque Central Illinois
March 3, 2007

A thing of beauty is a joy forever. John Keats

Driving home from St. Louis on Interstate 55 recently, I recalled my impression of central Illinois when I first traveled that route. As a college student riding a bus from Texas to Champaign on a snowy December day, I had looked at the stark, desolate countryside and thought to myself, "Who would ever want to live here?"

My impression changed completely when I moved to Lincoln in 1991. I now treasure the many picturesque scenes I've discovered throughout Logan County. Most look like they belong on an American-themed wall calendar.

Having lived in temperate climates most of my live, I especially enjoy the beauty of the seasons. Vibrant fall leaves and bright orange pumpkins provide a riot of color when autumn arrives.

Despite the hassles of winter weather, I like the

way ice-covered trees shimmering in the sunlight against a blue sky bathe the county in a magical aura and snowfalls transform the countryside into a fairyland appearance.

I'll never forget one day standing atop the sledding hill behind our house with my five-year-old son, enveloped by a silent, white world as snow softly swirled around us.

But despite the beauty of winter, I appreciate the colors of spring when they arrive. From crocus blossoms which sometimes peek up through the snow, to the profusion of tulips and daffodils, colors of the rainbow seem to burst forth in celebration of warmer weather.

Vivid yellow forsythia bushes brighten yards. Magnolia trees dress up in their dainty pink flowers. Blooming dogwood and redbud trees adorn wooded areas.

In summer, acres of verdant green fields of corn and soybeans — as far as the eye can see — reflect a calmness you can't find in the busy city.

Prairie sunsets fill the sky with shades of pink, orange and purple. As my 10-year-old nephew from Houston told me when seeing a sunset here last summer, "We just don't get sunsets like this at home."

I find wide-open spaces dotted with occasional farmhouses and barns more soothing than the harsh steel and concrete of skyscrapers.

Logan County has a myriad of scenic spots. The drive from Cornland to Lake Fork is picturesque, as is the drive from Mt. Pulaski into Elkhart, passing under the impressive old Elkhart Bridge.

Lazy, meandering creeks create miles of enchanting views. Kickapoo Park and Madigan State Park both have acres of beautiful wooded areas and meadows. Towering massive oaks adorn Memorial Park.

Elkhart Hill provides some of the county's most stunning scenery, especially when delicate bluebells and other wildflowers carpet the ground of the forested areas. Elkhart Cemetery, atop the hill, is charming with time-worn headstones interspersed among old stone buildings.

The baseball field at Elkhart School is my husband's and my favorite athletic field in the county because of its picturesque setting at the base of Elkhart Hill.

In the north part of the county, Bethel Church and its adjoining graveyard sit on a knoll, looking much like a scene from a movie set in the 1880's.

Towering grain bins, found in even the smallest communities, stand tribute to the affluence agriculture has brought to the county.

An abundance of impressive historic buildings enhance the county's beauty.

The 14-block Courthouse Square Historic District in Lincoln has the biggest concentration of such structures. The Logan County Courthouse majestically anchors the district, with its dome quietly standing guard over the county day and night. Surrounded by trees dressed in white lights, in winter the courthouse takes on a magical appearance.

The Post Office, City Hall, Lincoln Public Library and the Lincoln Depot are among the architectural treasures in the historic district. Other towns have their historic gems as well. Mt. Pulaski has its former 8th judicial circuit courthouse; Atlanta has its charming library and unique J.H. Hawes elevator and Middletown has the Knapp-Chestnut building and Stagecoach Inn.

Historic neighborhoods with tree-lined brick streets and charming older homes provide Normal Rockwell scenes throughout the county.

Other delightful scenes include the ornate entrance at Scully Park in Lincoln, along with its fountain, and the unique band shell at Latham Park. Freshly painted wall art dresses up old buildings in Atlanta and Lincoln, adding to their appeal.

No discourse on beauty in Logan County would be complete without mention of the breathtaking hot air balloons at the Lincoln Art and Balloon Festival. The brightly colored balloons fill the sky as they float over the countryside, enhancing the picturesque scenes that lie below.

I'm glad I've had the chance to explore Logan County over the years to dispel my first impression. This truly is a beautiful county.

Servant Leadership
September 4, 2004

If you want to be great, wonderful. But recognize that he who is greatest among you shall be your servant.
Dr. Martin Luther King, Jr.

A new striking piece of art in front of the Earl C Hargrove Chapel at Lincoln Christian College greeted those who attended the Salute to America concert there last evening.

The life-sized bronze statue, entitled "Divine Servant," depicts the Biblical account of Jesus washing the feet of his disciple Peter. It was given by an anonymous donor to honor Dr. James D. Strauss, retired Lincoln Christian Seminary theology professor.

In Biblical times, foot washing of sandal-wearing guests was a sign of hospitality. However, it was performed by menial servants, not peers and certainly not teachers. The disciples were shocked when Jesus washed their feet. His actions became a model of Christian humility.

The compelling statue not only depicts the attitude of servanthood emphasized at LCC, it also provides a visual reminder of servant leadership to the community as a whole.

"This art conveys a message about who we are," noted LCC President Keith Ray. "It epitomizes the kind of spirit we have here with students and faculty."

This emphasis on servanthood at LCC is evident in the seminary's annual commencement ceremonies. After receiving their diplomas, graduates are each given a towel with the seminary's logo.

Dean Emeritus Dr. Wayne Shaw, who initiated the practice more than 20 years ago, often told seminarians the towel was a reminder that they graduated not for arrogance, honor or prestige, but to go out and wash the feet of the world.

Beyond a religious setting, servant leadership is a philosophy embraced by cutting edge management specialists in both corporate and government settings, especially in light of numerous scandals.

Former AT&T executive Robert Greenleaf, who coined the phrase in the 1970's, describes a servant leader as one who makes sure other people's important needs are being addressed. Their priority as leaders is to serve people rather than to obtain power or wealth. They have persuasive power rather than coercive, manipulative power.

I've dealt with many elected officials in Logan County whose priority is what's best for the residents. They've been effective in their positions.

Yet, I've also encountered some local politicians more enamored with the prestige of being leaders than concerned about the community. They've been a stumbling block to progress.

The leadership style of elected officials impacts the future of Lincoln and Logan County. Greenleaf recognized that connection as well, noting that individual efforts, inspired by vision and a servant ethic, can make a substantial difference in the quality of society.

Servant leaders need to listen and have foresight, he said. Servant leadership encourages collaboration and trust.

In his book "Stewardship, Choosing Service over Self-Interest," Peter Block notes that too often institutions are governed by self-interest. In contrast, when the main commitment is to the larger community it reflects authentic service.

Focusing constant attention on the individual or a small team breeds self-centeredness and entitlement, he said. Elected officials should keep that warning in mind when dealing with certain chronic complainers who only want what benefits them directly rather than what's good for the city or county.

The new Community Builders organization exhibits an attitude of servant leadership as it seeks to serve the well being of Lincoln, Ray noted.

The group of about 20 local Christian leaders meets monthly to discuss pressing community needs and pray about those concerns. Elected officials have attended the meetings to share their ideas and the challenges they face.

The vision of the loose knit group is to be a Christ-centered leadership organization that helps form a positive, thriving community. The members hope to influence the city economically, politically and religiously.

Community Builders is sponsoring its first Community Prayer breakfast at 8 am next Saturday in the Laughlin Center at LCC. The focus will be prayer for church, community and country. The public is invited to attend.

Perhaps the Community Builders' efforts will result in more servant leaders coming forward to commit themselves to Lincoln and Logan County, helping create a better future for all residents.

Gut Value Connections
February 10, 2007

"Coming together is a beginning; keeping together is progress; working together is success." Anonymous

Sen. Barack Obama (D-Illinois) will announce today whether he will seek the U.S. presidency. Regardless of his decision, Obama's ability to excite Americans is similar to that of the last two men to occupy the Oval Office.

Both Bill Clinton and George W. Bush were able to make gut value connections with voters, according to the book "Applebee's America: How Successful Political, Business and Religious Leaders Connect with the New American Community" by Douglas Sosnik, Matthew Dowd and Ron Fournier.

"Values are what Americans want to see in a candidate . . . before they're willing to consider their politics," the authors said. "We call President Bush's tenacity and President Clinton's empathy gut values."

"Today two gut values dominate the political landscape," they said. "Success will come to any leader who appeals to the public's desire for community and authenticity."

Although both state representatives and both state senators representing Logan County — all Republicans — have noted Obama's liberal position on issues, those positions may not matter to voters.

"Voters don't pick presidents based on their positions on a laundry list of policies," the authors said. "Rather, policies and issues are mere prisms through which voters take the true measure of a candidate: Does he share my values?"

"Many who opposed the war in Iraq voted for Bush because they thought he had the gut values to keep him safe," they noted.

Obama definitely appeals to the public's desire for community.

In a message on his presidential exploratory website, Obama said, "We have to change our politics, and come together around our common interests and concerns as Americans.

"This won't happen by itself," he continued. "A change in our politics can only come from you; from people across our country who believe there's a better way and are willing to work for it."

"Pundits like to slice-and-dice our country into Red States and Blue States; Red States for Republicans, Blue States for Democrats," he said. "But I've got news for them ... We are one people, all of us pledging allegiance to the stars and stripes, all of us defending the United States of America."

Obama has aptly been called "Chicken Soup for the Democratic Soul" but his appeal is even greater than partisan politics.

When Obama spoke at Lincoln College shortly after his election to the U.S. Senate, he certainly connected with the large, receptive crowd packed into the gymnasium — both the students and community members.

This gut value connection isn't just related to politics, "Applebee's America" authors noted. Americans yearn for connections, after recognizing the emptiness of the 1990's affluence. Although they may not be connecting in traditional ways, such as joining established civic groups and churches, they're making their own connections.

The rally among many Illinoisans for the Chicago Bears as they played in last Sunday's Super Bowl was an example of people wanting to belong to something greater than themselves. Fans at the Lincoln Speedway are the same way.

"Across America, people are investing their time on their own terms to be part of self-organizing groups that make things happen — connecting online and offline, short term and long term, for the greater good or just for kicks," the authors said.

The popularity of the website www.meetup.com to connect people of similar interests is one example. Several Lincoln residents have joined various meetup groups based in Central Illinois. Another community website which focuses on community - www.craigslist.org - also has become popular.

"People have an insatiable hunger for community, connection and a higher purpose in life," the authors said.

"Whether people are using new technologies or more traditional channels, a new spirit of engagement is flourishing in America," the authors note.

In Lincoln evidence of this can be found in several recently formed groups. The Pets Without Partners organization is tackling the problem of abandoned pets.

The Route 66 Heritage Foundation of Logan County has taken on the enormous job of saving the old Mill restaurant on Route 66. A group of young people and adults have joined forces to build a skate park in Lincoln for use by youngsters on skateboards, BMX bicycles and roller blades.

Yearning for connectedness is especially strong in exurbs - small, prosperous communities situated beyond the suburbs of a city, the book noted. Most residents in those areas are strangers to each other, surrounded by big box retailers and chain restaurants that look the same in hundreds of other cities.

In Logan County, we're fortunate to have a sense of community with our small-town friendliness and uniqueness. Few other towns have as charming a downtown as the Courthouse Square Historic District in Lincoln, or a courthouse where Abraham Lincoln practiced law, like Mt. Pulaski or a smiley face water tower, like Atlanta.

Next month the Lincoln - Logan County Chamber of Commerce will be promoting the county to potential new residents at the Bloomington Home Show. Certainly our sense of community will be an attribute worth highlighting.

Dreams
April 1, 2006
(NOTE DATE)

Nothing happens unless first we dream. Carl Sandburg

The first of April has brought some remarkable new ventures to the city of Lincoln.

AL Telecommunications, a Fortune 500 company, has announced plans to build a 1.2 million-square-foot warehouse on Lincoln's north end.

AL is expected to hire 800 people with jobs paying from $25,000 to $55,000, for an average salary of $40,000.

Company officials selected Lincoln because the connection their CEO Willie Lincoln has to Abraham Lincoln.

"Being named for the son of our most beloved president, I've always been fascinated with Lincoln and his life," the founder explained. "What better place to build our new warehouse than the city christened by Abe. Of course, the city's central location and friendliness also make it an ideal choice."

Giggle, Inc., a leading children's software company, has agreed to terms with Lincoln officials on a site for its new corporate headquarters bringing 1,000 new jobs to Lincoln. Several tall buildings will be constructed including a recreation center with huge TV screens for test-marketing its computer software using local children as paid consultants. Over 250 children, ages five to 15, will be employed in the new facility.

Meanwhile, state officials have issued a press release detailing a new use for the former Lincoln Development Center property. Illinois Healthcare Inc. has committed to building an extensive medical complex on the site. In conjunction with the University of Chicago's medical school, the complex will include facilities for training physicians and doctors who work with developmentally disabled and geriatric patients.

A cancer center specializing in cutting-edge treatments also will be part of the complex. The LDC scenic campus appealed to cancer specialists who believe nature and the slower pace of small town life can speed cancer recovery.

Even more jobs will be created with the opening of the Lincoln Technical Training Center next fall. With hundreds of state-of-the-art computers, the center will train local students and adults in computer programming and software applications. A portion of the center also will house a technology center where data processing jobs from throughout the English-speaking world will be handled via the Internet.

The increase in jobs locally is expected to create a need for additional housing, especially after a recent tornado destroyed dilapidated homes on Fifth Street Road.

Later this month Sophisticated Properties will be asking the Lincoln Planning Commission for permission to build distinctive townhouses in downtown Lincoln. Located on the property currently housing the city garage on Kickapoo Street, the townhouses will have lofts overlooking Latham Park and nearby historic buildings.

To provide recreational opportunities for the new townhouse dwellers as well as long-time downtown residents, the Lincoln Area YMCA has decided to build its new facility on the site of the former Chicago Street garment factory. The "Y" expects the downtown location to allow many patrons to walk to the facility.

Also planned for downtown is an ambitious tourism venture unveiled by Main Street Lincoln and the Abraham Lincoln Tourism Bureau. With the concept of turning Lincoln into a historic destination like Galena, the project includes the rebuilding of the former Lincoln House Hotel into a small luxury hotel.

Entertainment also is part of the downtown tourism plan. After the Lincoln Theater builds its six-screen complex just west of its present location, the existing theater will be converted into the Central Illinois Arts Center. Musician Kenny G will kick off the center's first season.

An aggressive marketing campaign will tout Lincoln as the ideal location for weekend get-aways and business retreats. The Courthouse Square Historic District, with its excellent shopping and restaurants, will be featured.

The railroad is a key component in this project.

The new high speed train approved by federal officials will make Lincoln an attractive destination for Chicago and St. Louis residents. Local officials also will partner with railroad enthusiasts who have their own train cars.

With the anticipated increase in train traffic, the Lincoln Depot will be restored as a transportation center. Tourists who arrive by train will be able to take taxis or horse-drawn buggies to their downtown destinations.

Across town, the Logan County Fair Board has announced plans to relocate the fairgrounds to land north of the county airport. The move also will include building new state-of-the-art covered bleachers.

In preparation for the arrival of new residents with children, top school officials are proposing an agreement to consolidate the existing school districts into the Lincoln Consolidated School District. They expect the new district to operate more efficiently and with more flexibility.

The addition of new students has especially excited high school officials. Their enrollment will be up, eliminating the need to lay off teachers. They're also excited that the supervisor of the new AL Telecommunications warehouse has two teen-aged sons who are nationally-ranked football players. High school football boosters are hopeful these new athletes will lead the team to a winning football season and success in the play-offs.

By now you've probably realized that this column is an April Fools prank.

But these ideas aren't foolish. Rather, they're the dreams of several local community leaders which could be accomplished with a clear vision for the city's future and strong determination.

People

Moving Back
December 11, 2004

Home is a place you grow up wanting to leave, and grow old wanting to get back to. John Ed Pearce

A frequent lament among Lincoln residents is that their children don't return to Lincoln after completing their education.

However, some young adults are choosing to move back to Lincoln after living elsewhere.

Most relocate here to be closer to family. All consider Lincoln a desirable place to live.

Troy Brown, a 1992 Lincoln Community High School graduate, recently accepted a position with the Logan County Probation Office so he could live in Lincoln.

After graduating from Western Illinois University, Brown worked as a probation officer in Charleston for three years. When he found himself spending most weekends in Lincoln visiting family and friends, he decided to seek a probation position in town. A year and a half elapsed before one became available.

"I really enjoyed my experiences living elsewhere, but it just wasn't home," Brown said. "This is a great community with great people."

Patrick Doolin, a 1987 LCHS graduate, moved back to Lincoln in 1998 with his wife, the former April Davison, a 1988 grad. After Doolin sold his software company to a firm in Willmar, MN in 1992, the newlywed couple moved there. They lived in Minnesota six years, starting the Integrity Data business there.

After having children, the Doolins longed to be closer to family.

"We loved Minnesota and had great friends there, but the draw of family was greater than everything else," Doolin said.

Although Doolin could have based his software business anywhere, he chose Lincoln over surrounding cities to draw on the local workforce.

"We wanted to allow other people to work in a high-tech environment and still have the small-town life of Lincoln," he explained.

Doolin also moved to Lincoln to have input in its future, an opportunity he'll have as incoming president of the Lincoln/Logan Chamber of Commerce.

"Serving as chamber president wasn't my goal," he said. "The chamber was a vehicle to get to know people and how things work in the community. I've enjoyed the caliber of people here. There are some strategic thinkers on the chamber board, which made me more inclined to serve as president.

"When you move away, your eyes get opened to things that exist in Lincoln, whether good or bad. You become sensitive to the good things that you don't have elsewhere, and you bring good things from other places to help with problems here."

Despite the career success Doolin has experienced here, it's family connections he relishes most, with four children, Kyra, 8, Honna, 5, Adrianna, 4 and Luke, 2.

Bryan and Kendra Hartman lived in the Chicago area before moving back to Lincoln four years ago. Bryan, a 1993 LCHS graduate, worked as a land surveyor after the couple married in 1999. His wife, the former Kendra Locke who graduated from LCHS in 1994, worked as a radiation therapist when a position opened at Decatur Memorial Hospital. Bryan found a land surveyor position in Peoria a few months later.

"It's hard to make good friends in Chicago," Kendra noted. "We came here all the time to see friends and attend family functions."

"We didn't want to raise a family in Chicago," she said, noting they have a three-year-old daughter Hannah and an 18-month-old son Zane.

"Lincoln is a family-oriented town, good for little kids and good for young adults," she added. "It's easy to raise a family here. I feel safe and it's affordable."

Chris Bennett, a 1992 LCHS graduate, moved back to town with his wife Lesleigh nearly two years ago. They opened Bennett's Funeral Home last April.

After serving in the Marine Corps and receiving an associate's degree from the Mid-America College of Funeral Service, Bennett worked at Staab Funeral Home in Springfield for six years. He always intended to open a funeral home in Lincoln but waited for the right place at the right time.

The new funeral business and its location have worked out even better than the Bennetts hoped.

"We've been well received and we're happy being downtown," he said. "When you leave as a young person, you know certain people. When you move back, you get to know a whole new group of people."

"It's been great to be able to have time for family and church," Bennett said about being his own boss. He has a seven-year-old son Christian and a four-year-old daughter Kacey. He and Lesleigh are expecting a baby this month.

After seeing the world as a Marine and living in Springfield, Bennett said, "I'm happy to be here. I don't want to go anywhere else."

Adam May, a 1996 LCHS graduate, moved to Lincoln to help his brother in 2000, after interning in Chicago. He never left. With a degree in cinematography from Southern Illinois University, May opened his own photography business, AMP Studio, downtown. He married a fellow 1996 graduate, Sarah Bryant, who is technical director for Kirkland Fine Arts Center at Millikin University in Decatur.

"I wasn't looking forward to coming back," May said. "I thought I'd end up in Chicago as a corporate shooter. Family is the number one reason I'm here, but it's been a good spot for my business."

May noticed a slower pace in Lincoln than larger cities.

"There's time to stop and smell the flowers here," he said.

Tribute to Mike Abbott
November 11, 2006

The days we are given are gifts from above and today we remember to live and to love.

>   from "We Live" by Superchick

After the unexpected death of Mike Abbott at age 58 last week, some local residents probably made doctor appointments to assess their own health. Others gave their spouses an extra hug or two.

But Abbott had a far greater influence on the community. He truly made a difference in his hometown and in the lives of people who knew him.

Sometimes accountants are only interested in the bottom line. Abbott, founder of J.M. Abbott and Associates, was a clear exception to that stereotype.

He was a great asset to the Lincoln community with his commitment to improving the city and his ideas on how to accomplish that. His firm has provided top-notch professional accounting and investing services, with a quality equal to that of firms in larger cities.

Local organizations benefited from his professionalism and expertise, including the Abraham Lincoln Healthcare Foundation, Lincoln Elks Lodge 914, the First Presbyterian Church and the Woods Foundation.

Abbott was one of the first to invest money in downtown Lincoln before downtown revitalization became popular. In the late 1970's, he and dentist Larry Crisafulli remodeled the former Sears store into the Century Building.

I first met Mike at a meeting of the Main Street Lincoln Economic Restructuring Committee 12 years ago. I was impressed with his willingness to support downtown development based on educated speculation rather than relying only on solid numbers like most accountants.

Perhaps his greatest contribution to the community was his "out of the box" ideas.

Rob Orr, executive director of the Lincoln and Logan County Development Partnership, remembers Abbott's vision of what the city could be. After one Main Street committee meeting, Abbott walked with Orr to a business on land where a city park used to sit. He shared his idea of the city helping that business relocate and turning the property back into a park.

When the Lincoln Area YMCA discussed moving to the outskirts of town, Abbott stressed the importance of having the facility located downtown where it would be accessible to children arriving on foot or by bicycle.

Another of his ideas was to relocate the Logan County Fairgrounds to a rural site, which would minimize the impact of fairground events on residents and allow that ground to be developed.

In addition to his involvement in the community, Abbott had a big impact on the people who knew him.

At his memorial service last Sunday, several people shared how Abbott befriended them when they moved to Lincoln, making them feel at home here. Others talked about how he reminded his friends and clients to make their families a priority, a philosophy he put into practice. Some mentioned how Abbott enjoyed life.

He also was very close to his staff.

"It was like we were a family, and he was the dad," recalled CPA Debbie Last.

"He was very encouraging to us," she said, recalling a project he'd assigned her a few months ago.

"It was a stretch for me, but he kept saying 'you can do this'," she said.

Abbott's death reminded me of a poem I heard in church last Sunday entitled "The Dash" by Linda Ellis.

I read of a man who stood to speak at the funeral of a friend. He referred to the dates on her tombstone from the beginning to the end.

He noted that first came the date of her birth and spoke of the following date with tears, but he said what mattered most of all was the dash between those years.

For that dash represents all the time she spent alive on the earth and now only those who loved her know what that little line is worth.

For it matters not how much we own . . . the cars . . . the house . . . the cash. What matters most is how we live and love and how we spend our dash.

State Farm Agent Rick Hamm shared with me the

book "The Dash – Making a Difference with Your Life," based on the poem. He's so impressed with the book, he's been giving copies to friends and business associates in his usual encouraging way.

The poem suggests ways to have a meaningful life.

So think about this long and hard: are there things you'd like to change? For you never know how much time is left that can still be rearranged.

If we could just slow down enough to consider what's true and real and always try to understand the way other people feel.

And be less quick to anger and show appreciation more and love the people in our lives like we've never loved before.

If we treat each other with respect and more often wear a smile, remembering that this special dash might only last a little while.

So when your eulogy is being read with your life's actions to rehash, would you be proud of the things they say about how you spent your dash?

I think Abbott would have been proud of what was said at his memorial service. Maybe we need to follow his example and make service to the community and time with our families a priority as well.

Special Mothers
May 13, 2006

A mother is the truest friend we have. Washington Irving

Mother's Day is a time to reflect on the impact our mothers have had on us. The daughters of Becky Werth, Melody Shew and Kathleen Lowe all have been strongly influenced by their mothers.

Werth taught her daughter, DeAnn Cooper, about making wise choices and having good judgment.

"She set expectations for me and I didn't want to disappoint her," Cooper said. "She told me she'd trust me unless I showed her she couldn't."

"Mom got us out of bed on Sunday mornings for church, whether we wanted to go or not," she remembered. "I'm glad she paved that path for me. She's a great role model in that area."

"She also encouraged us to try out for any activity we were interested in and to go beyond our comfort zone," she added.

Living in Lincoln as an adult, Cooper is pleased her mother hasn't meddled in her life.

"Mom is so good at subtly making suggestions when I'm dealing with difficult situations," she noted. "I have to admit, most of the time she's right."

Cooper has fond childhood memories of her mother.

"She always made a big deal out of birthdays, and even made my birthday cakes in special shapes," she explained. "She also loved Christmas and decorated a lot."

Cooper remembers her mother traveling extensively with her and her younger brother Chris when they competed with the Lincoln swim team.

Family camping trips, which Werth organized for her children and her husband, Terry, were memorable, too. The family continues to camp together every year, with spouses and children in tow.

Angie Getchel learned patience from Shew, who is her boss at MKS Jewelers as well as her mother.

"She showed me how to be caring and compassionate," Getchel said. "She taught me to not compare my children, but to love them for who they are.

"Mom also taught me that marriage takes love and patience, and you should give it your best."

Raising children in a Christian home and putting God at the center of a marriage were other lessons Getchel learned from Shew.

"Throughout her lifetime, God has been at the forefront of our family, and a strong part of Mom's life, which has been a blessing to us," she said.

Getchel remembers Shew sewing dresses for her when she was growing up, a skill she had learned from her own mother, a professional seamstress.

Family vacations with her mom, her dad, Allen, and her brother, Mark were a highlight of Getchel's childhood. They traveled to historic places, including Mt. Rushmore, Yellowstone, New York and Washington, D.C.

"Now that I have kids, I can appreciate what they went through," she said.

Getchel also has special memories of attending mother/daughter banquets in Urbana with her mother, her aunt and her grandmother.

When she was 16, Getchel began working at the jewelry store before trying other ventures. Shortly before getting married in 1986, she came back to work for her mother.

"It's great for the most part, although there are some challenging days," she said. The two enjoy each other's company so much, they've arranged to both have Wednesdays off so they can do things together. Scrapbooking, water aerobics, ceramics and shopping are among their shared activities.

Working together also has been a key part of Katie Hoinacki's relationship with her mother. Lowe and her family operated Kathleen's Hallmark and Lighthouse Christian Bookstore for 32 years, until selling it a few months ago.

"Mom always had time for our family, even though we had a family business," Hoinacki said. That was no easy task, with seven children . . . Katie, Amy, Troy, Jennifer, Travis, Molly (who died as an infant) and

Emily.

"She always made holidays special, and continues to do so," Hoinacki said. "She threw birthday parties for us every two or three years. She's always full of surprises, like giving each of us mothers a framed photo of ourselves as children at a Mother's Day dinner last weekend."

Hoinacki began working in the store as a youngster, unwrapping cards and bagging customer purchases. In junior high she began running the cash register. As she and her siblings got older, they took over certain departments, with their father Virgil handling the bookkeeping.

"Working together was great," Hoinacki said. "We complemented each other in what we liked to do."

Since the shop sold, she's missed working with her mom, so she's recruited her to help her as a Mary Kay Cosmetics consultant.

Hoinacki has great memories of family vacations the Lowes took to attend Christian bookseller conventions.

"We went all over the U.S.," Hoinacki said, noting they enjoyed the kids programs at the conventions and meeting famous Christian authors and musicians.

Hoinacki learned from her mom that having the cleanest house is not as important as spending time with your children.

"I learned that the dust will wait," she said. "If you don't take the time with your children, they won't have the memories. They grow up so fast, enjoy them now."

"Mom also taught me that if you put God first, then family and then the business, it all balances out," Hoinacki said.

Memorable Fathers
June 18, 2005

My father didn't tell me how to live; he lived, and let me watch him do it. Clarence Budington Kelland

Many Lincoln residents were raised by committed and caring fathers who had a positive influence on them.

The sons of Bob Graue, Ron Schilling, Dom Dalpoas and Bob Olson are among the fortunate ones raised by such dads.

Time spent together on family trips created fond memories for Chris Graue, who operates the Graue Inc. car dealership his father founded.

"My dad always put his family first," Graue said. "He was busy with the dealership, but every year we'd take a family vacation." The Graues usually traveled in a camper, visiting places like Colorado and Niagara Falls.

The elder Graue has always had a positive attitude, his son said. He also dispensed a lot of wisdom.

"He always told me that when dealing with a spouse, don't let the sun set on your anger," Graue said. "He said you should settle your problems before the next day."

Graue also learned about operating a car dealership from observing his father.

"He always put himself in the customer's or employee's shoes," Graue said, noting that he tries to follow his dad's honest, ethical business practices.

Graue said his father's faith in God has played a major role in his father's life.

"I don't know how many times I heard him say, 'Thanks be to God,'" he said.

In addition to Chris, Bob and his wife Jody raised five other children: Barb Nickles and Mark who live in Lincoln, Beth who works in Madison, WI, Steve who works in Chicago and Tom, who passed away in 1990.

Tony Schilling appreciated the way his father Ron, recently retired Lincoln College president, stayed connected with the family, even on business trips.

"When my dad traveled, he'd bring us back something different from the cities he visited," Schilling said.

Schilling also has fond memories of family vacations.

"We'd always drive the station wagon with the wood on the side," he said of trips taken to Texas, Mississippi and North Carolina. "I'd ask questions all the time. I thought my dad knew it all.

"The time spent in those cars asking questions made me who I am today," he said.

"My dad is an all around nice, gentle man," Schilling noted. "People say how friendly he is and how he listens to people. In today's world, it's special for someone who has so many responsibilities to be able to do that."

Schilling appreciates his father's support over the years. "When I'd get discouraged, he'd always say 'you're doing fine'. He's a very optimistic person. I get that from him."

In his role as Lincoln College's executive director of enrollment management, Schilling applies much of what he observed from his dad.

"I've learned from him how to relish the mission of the school," he said. "Lincoln College is not about money or numbers, but about providing unique services for students who can use them."

Ron and his wife Joyce also raised two daughters, Kristin Klockenga, a local teacher, and Stacy who works in San Francisco.

The priority that Dom Dalpoas, director of the Oasis Senior Center, has placed on his family is greatly appreciated by his five sons, Dolan, Dakin and Dayne of Lincoln, Donta of Kokomo, IN and Devin of St. Louis.

They recall their dad spending time with them and enjoying life's simple pleasures like learning to ride a bicycle, going to a ballgame or sharing the birth of his five grandchildren. All five sons consider themselves "family guys" who enjoy time with loved ones.

"The most important advice he's passed on is 'family first,'" they said. "He believes in valuing family, because life passes by very quickly. At the end of the day, it's your family who will be behind you."

Dalpoas had other advice which influenced his sons. One was "if you start something, you finish it" which taught them to choose endeavors wisely and never,

ever give up, they said.

"The other advice was 'too much of any one thing is bad,'" they added. "This taught us balance and centeredness, and not to pursue one important venture at the expense of other equally important ones."

"Our dad is an honest, decent and hard-working human being who has sacrificed countless times to provide for his family," his sons said. "But we'd be remiss if we didn't mention how he cared for his parents as they passed on. The strength of character he demonstrated and the steadfast commitment to seeing their needs met above his own always will be special."

Jim Olson, son of former State Rep. Bob Olson (R-Broadwell), has fond memories of family vacations with his father.

"We'd take the pop-up camper and go places like Washington, D.C., Gettysburg and Mt. Rushmore," he said. "He showed us a lot of the United States."

With five children, things were hectic in the Olson household. Olson has a brother Bobby in Jacksonville, and three sisters, Sandy Tiffany in Lincoln, Nancy Courtwright in Broadwell and Susan Johnston in Mahomet.

"I'm sure there were lean times when we were kids, but we never knew it," he said. "As a farmer, he'd fret about the weather and bad markets, but didn't show it."

Olson appreciates his relationship with his father, especially when his father gave him the opportunity to come into the family farm operation.

"We see each other every day," he said. "He helps me out and listens to me. Most of the time, he's had that problem at some time. He's my dad and my teacher."

Inspiring Political Figures
October 30, 2004

Example is not the main thing in influencing others. It is the only thing. Albert Schweitzer

The presidential election Tuesday hopefully will determine the next president of the United States. Not only will this man have an impact at the national level, he also may influence many Americans.

Several local elected officials have been inspired by former U.S. presidents.

Illinois Native Ronald Reagan is one former president greatly respected locally.

"I was a sophomore at Eureka College - Reagan's alma mater - when he was running for president," noted Logan County Clerk Sally Litterly. "He came to speak at the college and was admired by all of us for his policies, good works and warm personality."

County Board Member Dick Logan also was inspired by Reagan.

"He could relate well to people," he said. "He tried to understand their problems and address them."

Reagan's common sense, along with his disregard for popularity polls, impressed Mt. Pulaski Mayor Bill Glaze. "Reagan said what he thought and people respected him for that."

As a high school student, Glaze took a day off school to see Reagan speak at the Illinois State Capitol during his 1984 campaign.

Glaze also admires Harry Truman who, although a Democrat, had similar characteristics as Reagan.

"His is a story most Americans can relate to," Glaze said. "Most of us remember the smile on his face in the photograph where he's holding the newspaper announcing the election of his opponent."

Truman and Reagan both were thrust into challenging foreign policy situations with little training yet performed very well, he added.

County Board Member Paul Gleason also admired Truman because he dared to make decisions including the removal of Gen. Douglas MacArthur.

John F. Kennedy is another revered president.

"We all thought JFK was a pretty darn good president," noted Logan County Board Chairman Dale Voyles.

Both Logan and Gleason were impressed with Kennedy's youthfulness and enthusiasm.

"Kennedy's administration opened a new era in America," Gleason observed. He was another president willing to make decisions such as during the Cuban Missile Crisis.

Voyles remembers talk about the strong leadership

of Harry Truman and Dwight Eisenhower from his childhood.

"They showed what leadership was with their strength and decision making," he said.

County Board Member Pat O'Neill admires former President Bill Clinton for the way he had a dream and went after it. Gleason also is attracted to Clinton's bubbly personality, while admitting the man has morality problems.

Not surprising for a local historian, Gleason also respected Abraham Lincoln, especially the speeches he gave with such limited formal education.

Former elected officials from Logan County also influenced current local leaders. Former U.S. Secretary of Agriculture Ed Madigan, who also served 18 years as a congressman, was greatly respected in his hometown of Lincoln.

Madigan was honest with people and gave them a fair shake, Logan remembered.

O'Neill admired the work Madigan did and the fact that he never forgot his roots.

"I'd see him at Holy Family Church and he'd go out of his way to see people," he recalled. "He really cared about people. He was truly respected and got a lot done. I've tried to pattern myself after him."

City Alderman Pat Madigan, nephew of the former congressman, has been directly influenced by his uncle as well as his father, former State Sen. Robert Madigan, and his grandfather, former Circuit Clerk and County Board Member Earl Madigan.

He recalled how his father, uncle and grandfather all could hold the attention of a roomful of people.

"When they spoke, people tended to listen," he said. "They could talk to people in all walks of life. They were willing to take into account everyone's views.

"They did such a good job for the community, I wanted to do the same," Madigan said of his decision to enter politics, although it meant overcoming a fear of public speaking.

Former County Treasurer Herman Dammerman had a great impact on current Treasurer Mary Ellen Bruns who worked for him for 18 years before being elected to the post herself.

"His whole attitude toward his job and dealing with people was very dignified," she recalled. "I learned a lot about how to approach the office from him."

Bruns also respected former County Clerk Pete Franz, noting his concern about people.

Circuit Clerk Carla Bender admired Martin Luther King, Jr. for his powerful convictions while she was growing up.

Former County Board Member Dick Hurley influenced Bender as her fifth grade teacher, while Gleason influenced her as her eighth grade Social Studies teacher.

Mayor Beth Davis greatly admires State Treasurer Judy Baar Topinka and former First Lady Barbara Bush. Topinka demonstrates the qualities of boldness, forthrightness and frugality, which are scarce in some female politicians, Davis said.

"Barbara Bush always struck me as a woman who never lived on pretense but what you saw is what you got," Davis said. "She is beautiful inside and out, one smart cookie, and so very much reminds me of my own mother."

Tribute to Sonya Twist
April 9, 2005

Inspiring people are vitamins for our spirits. They come in all kinds of disguises and descriptions. Sark

Sonya Twist, the Lincoln Community High School sophomore killed in an auto accident a week ago, is being remembered as a young woman who was extraordinarily talented and full of life. Her impact on the lives of others is incredible.

Sometimes the way people remember a young person who dies has little resemblance to how he or she actually lived. Not so with Twist.

More than 400 community members, most of them teenagers, attended her Celebration of Life at Lincoln Christian Church Wednesday. Her visitation will be 4-7 pm Monday at the church's fellowship center with the funeral at 10 am Tuesday in the church sanctuary. Graveside services will be in Washington that afternoon.

Twist was very accomplished musically, with a

passion for playing the French horn. She was first chair in French horn in the LCHS Band where Director David Swaar selected the band's music to showcase her talent. He predicted she could have reached her goal of becoming a professional musician. Twist was returning from French horn lessons with a University of Illinois professor when her fatal accident occurred.

Public speaking was another area of Twist's expertise. She was a member of the LCHS Speech Team where she was selected most outstanding freshman last year. She was part of the Group Interpretation team which earned sixth place in state competition. She also was narrator in the Performance in the Round production of "Horton Hears a Who", which took first in both sectional and regional competition.

Despite her remarkable abilities, Twist is most remembered for her enthusiasm and love of others.

"She had raw energy," said Tracy Thomas, youth director at Lincoln Christian Church, where Twist was an active member. "She was a little ball of thunder."

"She lived her life almost as if she knew her time was short," he said. "She lived for the moment and she lived for God. She touched so many people as a result."

"The thing that struck us about Sonya when we met her as a freshman was her vibrancy," noted Ed Jodlowski, LCHS speech coach. "She had a glow about her and made sure everyone else in the room had it, too."

"Sometimes I'd go home and realize I liked life a lot better for having worked with Sonya that day," he added.

"She was so much fun to be around," said Swaar. "She was a great, great kid."

"Sonya was really crazy and spontaneous," said Hannah Snyder, an LCHS sophomore who was friends with Twist since preschool. "She didn't put on a false front. She was herself.

"She had a lot of energy and enjoyed life. She knew every day was important. She didn't take things for granted, especially the people she loved."

Twist's unselfishness and concern for others were evident to those who knew her.

"Sonya befriended and welcomed everyone," Thomas said. "She respected them for who they were. When she spoke to you, she treated you like you were the most important person in the world.

"With all she had going on, I don't know how she had time to do it," he said, remembering that on the day Twist died she spent three hours walking dogs with his daughter.

"Sonya had problems of her own, like everybody does, but you wouldn't know it because she cared about everyone else's problems," Snyder said.

Tim Searby, minister of worship at Lincoln Christian Church, recalls that Twist was the first student to seek him out after his diagnosis of prostate cancer.

"She'd check with me every week," he said. "She was so sweet and genuine. She really exemplified Christ here on earth."

"She was kind to everyone she met and was always giving hugs," said LCHS Senior Eric Knutilla, who Twist referred to as her big brother. "I only heard her say one unkind thing about someone and that was just that they were annoying.

"She was one of the greatest people I ever met," he

said. "She changed my life for the better. She'll really be missed."

"Sonya was one of those rare individuals who thought more of others than herself," Swaar noted. "When she forgot her French horn at the national competition in Indianapolis, she didn't feel bad for herself. She felt bad that she had let everyone down.

"We know she's playing in a better band now."

"Anyone who knew her realized Sonya was one of a kind," observed Todd Parmenter, minister of administration at Lincoln Christian Church.

The church fielded hundreds of calls about Twist from across central Illinois after the accident, including students she'd befriended at band and church camps.

"There's always an outpouring of grief with an untimely death, but this is beyond that, tenfold," Parmenter said. "The level of grief is deeper than you'd expect. It's more than people putting themselves in the parents' shoes, but rather experiencing grief themselves because they'll miss her."

"Sonya had an eternal perspective on life," Thomas said. "She was in love with God and now she is with him."

"If students were to imitate Sonya like she imitated Christ, the high school and community of Lincoln would never be the same," Thomas said.

Helping Our Soldiers
September 25, 2004

Pick up my gun an' get back to work...an' it keeps me driving me on, waiting on letters from home.
                    John Michael Montgomery song

Loneliness. Boredom. Round-the-clock danger. These are among the challenges facing American soldiers serving in Afghanistan and Iraq.

Several Logan County groups and individuals are trying to make life easier for these men and women.

Veterans of Foreign Wars Post 1756 is contributing money to Operation Uplink which provides pre-paid phone cards to military personnel. They're also sending donations to the USO to help fund USO overseas shows for U.S. troops.

American Legion Post 263 is selling magnetic patriotic ribbons with proceeds going to the Illinois National Guard support program for overseas troops and their families.

Christmas care packages are being complied by Rachelle Nelson, who's mailed care packages to U.S. soldiers for several months. She sends toiletries such as toothbrushes, soap and deodorant.

Nelson also sends food, which must be wrapped separately so as it doesn't absorb the smell of the toiletries. The soldiers' food is bland, so they appreciate anything with flavor, she said. She can't send perishable food, including chocolate and jerky, because it can take as long as three months to arrive.

One soldier wrote her of his appreciation for a care package. He said it arrived just as he was heading out to guard duty in the middle of the night.

"I tore into it like a kid at Christmas," he said. "I stuffed the candy in my pockets to take on duty."

Sending packages to soldiers helps take the burden off families to send so much to their loved ones, Nelson said.

Pam Ridgeway, whose son Jonathan Barton has spent time in Iraq as an Army lieutenant, sends phone cards and greeting cards to soldiers whose names she's collected from members at Jefferson Street Christian Church.

Most military bases in Iraq have phone service, although there can be long lines to use the phone, she said. Telephone calls from remote locations can eat up a lot of minutes, she added.

"We want the soldiers to know that we're praying for them and thinking about them," Ridgeway said.

Having sent packages and cards since her son went to Iraq at the beginning of the war, she's received numerous thank-you notes from soldiers.

"Some are heart-wrenching," she said.

The sixth grade class at Zion Lutheran School is selling Support our Troops and Pray for our Troops yellow ribbon magnets for $5 with the proceeds going for a homecoming party for A Company of the 1-106th Aviation Battalion. Sixth grader Bethany Last's father, David, is a helicopter pilot serving in Iraq with that battalion.

The school also is collecting items to send Last for a project unofficially called Operation Candy Drop. American crews in helicopters flying at low altitudes toss out large plastic bags filled with hard candies and soft toys to groups of children. The youngsters there have so little, these gifts are greatly appreciated, noted his wife Debbie, who will be sending care packages to her husband and his buddies.

"The soldiers really love to hear 'thanks for what you are doing,'" she noted.

The Rev. Mark Thompson, who served as a vicar at Zion Lutheran Church in Lincoln during his seminary studies, is currently a chaplain in Iraq. When members of Zion Lutheran Church in New Holland saw photos of how bare his chapel in Iraq was, they sent him colorful green paraments for the altar and lectern.

Zion, Lincoln church members currently are collecting items to mail him and soldiers in his unit. In addition to snack food and toiletry items, they'll be sending playing cards, paperback novels, small board games and DVDs to help combat the boredom.

When the church sent a package to Lincoln resident Brett Dellow during his tour of duty in the Midlde East last Spring, someone included 3,000 toothpicks, said Sunday

School Superintendent Peggy Meyer, who coordinated the project. They were put to good use by a soldier who used them to build a miniature bridge, she said.

Providing items for soldiers not only lets them know they're remembered at home, it's appreciated by families left behind who have their own struggles.

"I have a lot of help with the things I need," Last said, noting it took awhile to learn to call someone when she needed something.

"The biggest challenge is loneliness," she said. "He's my best friend."

LCHS Teacher Retirements
May 29, 2004

A teacher affects eternity; he can never tell where his influence stops. Henry Adams

After inspiring students for decades, four of Lincoln Community High School's best teachers are retiring this Spring.

Steve Sauer, Rita Vaught, Mitzi Welsh and Ida Johnson all are leaving teaching to pursue other interests.

Sauer, chairman of the Social Studies Department, has taught history at LCHS for 35 years. He has a reputation for being one of the hardest teachers at the school, yet one students appreciate later in life.

Comments from surveys of LCHS graduates reflect this.

"I worked hardest in Mr. Sauer's History and Psychology classes," wrote one student. "He made you earn your grades and was fair but tough."

"Mr. Sauer was strict," said another. "He helped prepare me for college the most."

Jonathan Parker, a 1986 LCHS graduate with a master's degree in history and a job in national politics, found Sauer uncompromising as a teacher. "Unlike so many teachers these days, he was very stingy with an 'A'," Parker said. "He wasn't about to let the mediocrity of a certain class set his grading curve. He made you earn it.

"One of his most challenging assignments was to hand out a newspaper article on a current event and make the students write summaries of the article and a critical analysis of the issue. Those were the hardest assignments I ever had in high school, but nothing prepared me more for college."

"His was one of the only classes I was really challenged in," noted Kyle Pepperell, a 2001 graduate studying theater at Ball State University. "He graded hard. His world history class definitely helped prepare me for college."

"Sauer's class was very intense," said Chris Meyer, a 2001 graduate who's majoring in history at Illinois State University. "When I decided to become a history teacher, I wanted to model myself after him."

"I remember how unfair I thought it was for my dad to make me take Mr. Sauer as a freshman when my friends chose not to have him as a teacher because he was too tough," observed Aaron Freesmeier, a 2001 graduate attending Spring Hill College in Mobile, AL.

"Now as a junior at a very difficult college where writing, homework and research are criteria upheld the most, I look back and am glad Mr. Sauer was part of my early high school days."

Pursuing a career chosen as a high school senior, Vaught taught in New Holland-Middletown for 16 years before coming to LCHS as an English teacher in 1988.

At LCHS she was part of the Teacher Leadership Academy. A staunch support of extracurricular activities, Vaught served as advisor to the LCHS Future Teachers of America club.

"Ms. Vaught taught me many different aspects of the English language but I remember much more her insights on life," recalled Laura Baker, a 2002 graduate currently studying anthropology at DePauw University. "As sophomores, my class and I felt life was so hard. Yet with a glimmer in her eye, she would smile and tell us it will only get harder. She taught me that any problem can be solved with a sense a humor."

"Rita Vaught is easily among the best teachers I had at LCHS," noted Sara Baker Netzley, 1995 valedictorian. "She actively fostered discussion in class about the day's lesson, which gave her students experience in the type of lively discourse common in college classrooms.

"She wasn't a teacher who commanded the class' attention by raising her voice. She was more mellow, with a subtle sense of humor that was worth shutting up and listening to hear.

"She was very encouraging of my own writing, which led me to seek out a career first as a journalist and now as a Ph.D. student hoping to teach journalism to college students someday," Netzley added.

Mitzi Welsh has taught biology at LCHS for 30 years, the last two as department chairman. She organized the school's LEAF environmental club and has served as its sponsor for more than a decade.

"Everyday has been a new adventure," Welsh noted. "I tried to keep biology interesting, challenging and up-to-date. I tried to be fair and teach students to be responsible."

"Mrs. Welsh was more like a college professor than I ever knew," Baker said. "Her calm, steady way of teaching was perfect in the chaotic realm of high school. She brought up challenging issues and encouraged us to examine a problem from all directions. She took the fear out of science for me."

Johnson, 1987 Jaycee Teacher of the Year and 2004 LCHS Teacher of the Year, was hired to teach special education at LCHS in 1971.

"I wasn't sure about this job," Johnson said, noting she didn't know much about special ed until taking additional classes. "It wasn't long before I began to love the students. They were honest, hardworking, loyal to those they loved, but in need of success. Every time I'd see the face of a child change after he or she accomplished the impossible, I was hooked for another year."

"Mrs. Johnson was one of my favorite teachers," noted Ross Green, a 2002 graduate who's studying law enforcement at Western Illinois University. "She was one you could talk to about anything and she'd understand. She was never opinionated but rather gave you reasons why you might consider something."

"Ida has always shown a love and concern for young adults and has made a positive difference in the lives of learning disabled students," noted Judy Rader, fellow special ed teacher. "She's been instrumental in directing post-secondary plans of students whether they were planning to join the work force or continue their education. She's definitely leaving a hole in the department."

These outstanding teachers will be missed.

Stay-at-home Moms
January 10, 2004

Being a stay-at-home mom is the hardest job there is.
Oprah Winfrey

In the movie "Mona Lisa Smile," Julia Roberts plays an art teacher who encourages bright young college women in the 1950s to consider goals beyond getting married and raising a family.

Much to her surprise, a woman who applied to law school decides to get married and raise a family instead. She explains she would definitely regret neglecting her family more than she might regret setting aside her corporate ambitions.

Fifty years later, women are still wrestling with balancing work and family. Although women are no longer expected to limit their goals to being wives and mothers, many are finding staying home with their children their most fulfilling option. Lincoln women are no exception.

Angie Whiteman was director of student activities at Lincoln College when her son Kameron was born 19 months ago.

"I was very adamant about going back to work after he was born," she remembered. But once he arrived, she hated the idea of leaving him while she went to work. Eight months later she left her Lincoln College position to be a full-time mother.

"Here I was helping these young people at the college, and I wanted to help my young person," Whiteman explained. Being home with her son has been awesome, she said.

"Once you have kids, your priorities change," she reflected, noting she's had to give up certain things. Her husband Kirk is a full-time professor at Lincoln College, as well as assistant basketball coach and head women's golf coach. They have a second child on the way.

"I don't want to be superwoman and do everything halfway," she observed.

Lisa Madigan was working as a paralegal in Springfield when she became pregnant six years ago. Once her daughter Teran was born, both she and her husband Pat felt it was important for her to stay home although it meant cutting their income in half. Pat works as a claims representative for State Farm Insurance and serves on the Lincoln City Council. A second daughter, Carson, was born two years ago.

Lisa admits there are days so stressful she'd like to put on a suit and go sit at her office desk. But she appreciates the benefits of staying home.

"People assume you want to be home to hear your child's first word or see their first step, which I did," she said. "But if I was at work I'd also miss the little things that come with seeing life through your child's eyes. I also like being there to instill my values in my children."

Mary Sager, an RN, worked as an education coordinator at Abraham Lincoln Memorial Hospital when 11-year-old Josh was born. She cut her hours to just a few a month to allow her be home with him and Caleb, who was born five years later. Her husband Andy works for the state of Illinois in Springfield.

"Andy felt I was the best one to take care of the kids," she explained. "No one loves your kids the way you do."

"I've enjoyed being there for them everyday," she said, noting they especially like going to the library or the park.

"It's a very small time frame until they grow up," she observed. "It's been a sacrifice to stay home, but I've never regretted it, ever."

Jody Nettles, who has an accounting degree, worked full-time until her eight-year-old son Henry was born. She now stays home with him and his younger brothers, Clayton, 6, and Levi, 4. Her husband Curt is principal at Lincoln Junior High.

"I like being here to do things with my boys and help at their school," she explained. "And I have time to fix meals so we can sit down to supper every night. I don't have to rush home from work."

Shannon Willmore was a case worker at Catholic Charities before deciding to stay home with five-year-old daughter Hailynn and a 14-month-old foster child.

"We figured it out financially and made it work," Willmore said. Her husband Matt is a sales manager for a medical equipment company.

"I love being with them every possible minute," she said, noting she'd always wanted to stay home when she became a mother. "I'm amazed at how quickly they change. I'm seeing them do new things every day."

"I rock the baby to sleep for her nap every afternoon," Willmore said. "We do a lot of baking and cooking, which I didn't do when I was working. I don't feel rushed like I used to. I'm so glad we made this decision."

All five women have found most friends and acquaintances are supportive of their decision to stay home.

"I haven't noticed the Mommy Wars in this town," Sager said. "Everyone has a different situation."

"Friends and co-workers have been so supportive, better than I thought," Whiteman said. "It's an individual decision. I'm glad to have a choice."

"I don't think people look down on me for staying home," Nettles echoed.

Initially Madigan found some resistance to her decision.

"A female attorney I worked with was shocked when I decided not to come back to work," she remembered. "None of my working friends had kids, so they were surprised. People assumed I'd go back to work."

"But I've made new friends," she said. "As a mom, your priorities and interests change, so your friends change."

Lincoln's "Idols"
August 13, 2005

Acting is a question of absorbing other people's personalities and adding your own experience.
Paul Newman

Entertainers in the American Idol concert I attended in St. Louis earlier this week impressed me with their talent, just as they had on their weekly TV show.

Yet as I watched the winning contestants perform, I couldn't help but think proudly of Lincoln's pool of extremely talented young performers.

Lincoln's young adults may not win nationwide competitions, but they've given local audiences stellar performances over the years. I've compiled my own Lincoln Idol list drawn from phenomenal Lincoln Community High School productions in the six years my kids have been students there.

One of the best LCHS shows I've seen was the 2000 spring musical "Guys and Dolls." Mastery of comedy and romance was evident among the strong ensemble of LCHS students.

The charm and finesse the student actors brought to their roles were so engaging that we found the St. Louis Muny performance of "Guys and Dolls" last year paled in comparison.

Nick King was ideal as the suave Sky Masterson in the LCHS production. Equally captivating was Ann Elliott as the Salvation Army missionary he woos. Their Havana scene was terrific, especially Elliott's uninhibited rendition of "If I Were a Bell" and their duet "I've Never Been in Love Before."

John Swanson had us laughing throughout the show as floating crap game organizer Nathan Detroit. Swanson brought the perfect combination of conman and earnestness to the role.

But it was freshman Betsy Buttell, who played his long-suffering finance Adelaide, who stole the show in her LCHS debut. She was masterful in the comedic role of the ditzy show girl. Buttell and Swanson's talent was especially evident in the song "Sue Me."

The "Guys and Dolls" supporting cast was topnotch as well. Kyle Pepperell and Abby Gerdts, who had many outstanding roles in their four years at LCHS, were super as Nicely-Nicely Johnson and a Salvation Army lieutenant. Josh Twente was wonderful as crapshooter Big Julie, a role which convinced him to study theater in college.

Pepperell showed the depth of his dramatic expertise as the teenage Honza in the haunting Holocaust play "I Never Saw Another Butterfly" six months later. In the same production Allyson Leonard was incredible as

Raja Englanderova, one of few youngsters who survived the Terezin concentration camp. The passionate realism she brought to the role was spellbinding.

Pepperell and Leonard teamed up again in the exceptional production of the 2001 spring musical "Oklahoma!", playing Curly and Laurie with great onstage chemistry. In the same show Kirsten Knutilla was a charming Aunt Eller and Buttell a delightful Ado Annie.

The 2002 fall play "A Curious Savage," a comedy set in a mental institution, showcased Buttell's talent along with that of Doug Rohrer, Ty Sank and Allison Kessinger. Brandon Davis stole the show with just one spoken line and a heartfelt hug.

"Savage" also introduced LCHS audiences to Lindsey Boerma's fine comic instincts and Brian Welter's southern drawl.

Buttell and Rohrer gave memorable performances in the 2003 spring musical "Joseph and Amazing Technicolor Dreamcoat," with Buttell as narrator and Rohrer as Joseph.

The Neil Simon comedy "Rumors" a few months later allowed Kasey Pepperell, Patrick Perry, Tom Swanson, Amanda Perry, Rohrer, Boerma and Davis to demonstrate how funny they can be onstage. Brady Gerdts was especially hilarious.

The 2004-2005 school year brought three first-rate productions to the LCHS stage beginning with the fall play "Noises Off". The farce required impeccable comic timing carried off incredibly well by Davis, Boerma, Swanson, Gerdts, Perry, Muck, Pepperell and Rachel Kasa. I was amazed that high school students could pull off a complicated show so well.

Switching from comedy to serious acting, a handful of LCHS students showed remarkable depth in the poignant winter play "Boys Next Door." Gerdts, Davis, Daniel Ohmart, Tony Curcuru and Janel Filbeck gave incredible performances as developmentally disabled individuals. Portraying their characters with realism and dignity, they gave the audience a glimpse into the hearts and minds of the mentally challenged. Eric Knutilla also did a great job as their social worker.

The school year ended with an exceptionally fine production of "Fiddler on the Roof" as the spring musical. Welter, who'd shown great talent as slow-speaking southern men, took the role of Tevye and made it his own in a unique portrayal of the Jewish father trying to hold his family together through troubled times in Russia.

Ruth Ohmart delivered a fine portrayal of his wife Golde and Kelly Lohrenz was impressive as daughter Hodel in the same production.

Lincoln can be proud to have high caliber young entertainers. This school year, make a point to see LCHS productions. No doubt Boerma, Curcuru and Filbeck will bring quality performances to the stage, along with their fellow Thespians.

Illinois State Fair
August 12, 2006

It's dollars to donuts that our state fair is the best state fair in our state.
    Lyrics by Oscar Hammerstein from "State Fair"

"Experience It!" is the slogan for the 2006 Illinois State Fair.

Hundreds of Logan County residents will experience the fun and festivities at the fair in the next couple of weeks. Some will experience a different aspect of the fair, though.

Dozens of volunteers from across the county work at the fair to earn money for their organizations. The Mt Pulaski High School Booster Club, the Oasis Senior Center and local Future Farmers of America chapters all have jobs at the fair.

Some local young people also travel to the fair to earn money working at the Guzzardo's food booths.

The MPHS Boosters Club has provided tram

service to fair visitors for more than two decades, according to David Meister, co-organizer of the operation along with Jeff Clements.

Using tractors rented from Cross Brothers Implement, volunteers operate seven trams throughout the fairgrounds from 8 am to 9 pm every day of the fair. They also have an eight-seat golf cart to transport senior citizens from the Illinois Building to the tram ticket booth near the Diary Barn.

Such a large undertaking requires 72 volunteers a day - 36 per shift, including drivers, ticket sellers and vehicle maintenance workers.

Several Mt. Pulaski groups in addition to the booster club send volunteers, such as American Legion and Rotary Club, Meister said. People from Mt. Pulaski, Chestnut, Elkhart, Cornland and Lake Fork pitch in, he added.

"We're fortunate to have an implement dealer right here in town," he said. "And we can pull in farmers to drive the tractors."

The booster club and other participating organizations share in the proceeds. Last year the Illinois Soybean Association began providing soy-based diesel fuel for the tractors in exchange for publicity, which has helped keep expenses down, Meister noted.

Also earning money for their organization are Oasis Senior Center volunteers who run daily bingo games in the Illinois Building. Eight people travel to the fairgrounds in the Oasis van - every day except the last Sunday - to staff the bingo games from 11 am to 5 pm.

Bingo players pay $1 per card. The prize is half the take minus taxes, which allows the Oasis to make a decent profit, said Oasis Director Dominic Dalpoas.

Some Oasis volunteers go every day since they enjoy the food and festivities of the fair, Dalpoas said.

The Illinois Building is air conditioned with no smoking, which makes a big difference for the volunteers, he added.

The bingo games generate a constant flow of people. Senior Day — on Monday of the fair — attracts the biggest crowd, Dalpoas said.

Darlene Freeman, the volunteer bingo manager, knows bingo frontwards and backwards, he said.

Local high school ag students tackle a less pleasant job to raise funds for their FFA chapters. They clean out the barns which house various animals during the fair.

The FFA chapters at Hartsburg Emden High School, Lincoln Community High School and MPHS each obtain a three-day or four-day contract with fair officials for barn clean-up. The students work from 8 pm until about midnight either hauling debris in a wheelbarrow to a dumping area or piling it in the center aisle.

The Hartsburg Emden chapter takes at least 10 students and two adults for barn cleaning.

"It's hard work," noted Betsy Pech, Hartem FFA advisor. "You're gonna sweat and you're gonna get dirty.

"You do it as a fundraiser," she explained, noting the club earns $500 a day.

"It beats selling candy door-to-door," she added.

Some of the ag students also volunteer at the Pork Patio operated by the Illinois Pork Producers across from the Grandstand, Pech said. Organizations provide 17 workers for two shifts - 10:30 am to 3 pm and 3-8 pm.

They wrap sandwiches and wait on customers,

Pech said.

"We did it for the first time last year and the kids had a ball," she said, noting the kids especially liked being able to eat at the Pork Patio for free.

Hardworking Logan County teenagers also can be found working at one of Guzzardo's three booths in the Food-a-rama located in the middle of the fairgrounds.

The restaurant employs 30 young people to work at the pizza, tenderloin and hamburger stands, transporting them daily by van. They work from 11 am to 9 pm, with breaks in the afternoon.

"It's hard work, but it's fun," noted Frankie Guzzardo.

"The kids are always great to work with," she said. "We've been fortunate to hire young people who are great workers.

"It's a family atmosphere working together, with lots of laughter."

The first Saturday is the biggest day of the fair, she said. The success of each year's fair hinges on that day, she added.

Having sold food at the fair for 37 years, the Guzzardos have the logistics down pat. A semi truck delivers food every day. Prairie Farms Dairy brings in ice cream for milk shakes daily, too.

Rib-eye sandwiches are great sellers on Saturdays and Sundays, while pizza is the best seller in the evenings, Guzzardo said.

It's hard-working people like these Logan County residents who help make the Illinois State Fair a great experience for attendees.

Help with Tornado Clean-up
June 7, 2003

The impersonal hand of government can never replace the helping hand of a neighbor. Hubert H. Humphrey

The willingness of Logan County residents to help when there's a need was clearly evident this week with the response to last Friday's tornados.

Numerous firefighters and sheriff deputies, along with Emergency Services Disaster Agency officials, arrived after the evening storm hit, checking on people and damage. The Logan County Sheriff's Auxiliary patrolled the area all weekend to prevent looting.

Vast volunteer clean-up efforts began Saturday morning when friends, family, neighbors and church members showed up Saturday morning to clear debris from the tornados. They arrived with work gloves, chainsaws, backhoes and tractors, jumping right in.

"We didn't need to tell anyone to go. They just went," said Dan Fulscher, county ESDA director. "No one got upset. They just asked what they could do."

There was plenty of devastation with more than $2 million in damage and at least 15 farms hit by tornado winds up to 170 mph.

Helpers removed furniture and other belongings from homes left uninhabitable by the storm. They combed fields for debris, piling it in the ditches for later pick-up by Department of Corrections crews. Fallen limbs were removed from buildings and vehicles. Rodney Molt from Molt Tree Service volunteered his time to remove trees felled by the storm.

"I knew I had good neighbors, but wow," said Bridget Schneider, whose recently renovated farm house was destroyed by the tornado. "I couldn't believe it when everyone came to help us. The response has been absolutely fantastic."

Schneider herself showed community commitment by handing out diplomas as a Lincoln Community High School board member at the LCHS graduation the night after the tornado devastated her home.

"People's response has been tremendous," said Ed Voyles, whose home also was demolished by the tornados. "Within two hours of the storm we had 40 or 50 people show up. Even the sheriff came by."

Not only did people come the next day with equipment to help with the physical work, they also provided food and beverages all weekend for those working, he said.

"You couldn't ask for better people," he added.

"I was overwhelmed when 50 people showed up to help Saturday," echoed Kim Beavers who lost a car shed, part of a barn and numerous trees. "I thought maybe a dozen would arrive, but not 50. I couldn't believe it.

"It was very encouraging to know I didn't have to do things alone," she added. "We got almost all the work done on the first day."

"The day after the storm we had people stopping by to help that we didn't even know," said Dennis Bruns, who lost a barn and machine shed to the tornado. "The community really opened their arms to us."

Volunteers cleaned up the mess in one spot and moved on to the next, noted Shirley Dittus, whose property received minimal damage. "It was wonderful to see people working together."

John and Sherry Fulton were among those who helped, providing Sunday night supper for all the affected families and crews, even delivering food to those who couldn't come.

"It's neighbors helping neighbors," Fulton explained. "You'd sure appreciate it if it were you."

Not only did volunteers provide physical labor, but also emotional assurance that people cared and would do whatever they could, Fulton added.

"The number of people who went to each home was incredible," Fulscher said. "We had as many as 80 people in one area at a time."

"The citizens of Logan County have always had wonderful hearts," he said. "Last weekend showed it one more time.

"This was one of the best orchestrated efforts of people doing things on their own I've seen," he said. "Because of their calm approach they got things done quickly."

ESDA's response to the tornado has been praised

by those affected.

"ESDA was fantastic," Schneider said. "I called 911 on my cell phone from a nearby ditch after we escaped from our basement when we smelled gas. ESDA was there within a matter of minutes. It made us feel better to have calmer heads helping us get to safety. They also stopped by several times over the weekend to keep us apprised of what was going on."

Not only did residents assist with the clean-up, they have been bighearted with those hard hit by the damage.

"People's generosity has been overwhelming," Schneider said. "We've received gift certificates for food, and even one to Kathleen's Hallmark so we could replace some knick-knacks. When I picked up our food order at a local restaurant this week, they wouldn't even let us pay. This is a great community."

"They say people in this area pull together like no where else," Dittus said. "I believe it."

For More Information About Lincoln, Illinois

Located in Information Station
1555 Fifth Street, Lincoln, IL 62656:

**Lincoln/Logan County
Chamber of Commerce**
www.lincolnillinois.com   217-735-2385

**Lincoln & Logan County
Development Partnership**
www.LincolnLogan.com   217-732-8739

**Abraham Lincoln Tourism
Bureau of Logan County**
www.abe66.com   217-732-8687

Located downtown
Main Street Lincoln
229 S. Kickapoo St. Lincoln, IL 62656
www.mainstreetlincoln.com   217-732-2929

For information on the Route 66 Heritage Foundation of Logan County go to
www.savethemill.org